# BRIDGE OF DREAMS

# BRIDGE OF DREAMS

## THE REBIRTH OF THE BROOKLYN BRIDGE

### PHOTOGRAPHS BY BURHAN DOGANÇAY

WITH AN INTRODUCTION BY PHILLIP LOPATE

HUDSON HILLS PRESS　　　　　NEW YORK

Published in the United States by Hudson Hills Press, Inc.,
122 East 25th Street, 5th Floor, New York, NY 10010-2936.

Distributed in the United States, its territories and possessions, and
Canada by National Book Network.

Distributed in the United Kingdom, Eire, and Europe by
Art Books International Ltd.

Editor and Publisher: Paul Anbinder

Manuscript Editor: Phil Freshman

Proofreader: Lydia Edwards

Designer: Betty Binns

Composition: Angela Taormina

Manufactured in Japan by Toppan Printing Company.

LIBRARY OF CONGRESS CATALOGUING-IN-PUBLICATION DATA

Dogançay, Burhan, 1929–
    Bridge of dreams : the rebirth of the Brooklyn bridge / photographs by
Burhan Dogançay ; essay by Phillip Lopate.
        p.    cm.
    ISBN: 1-55595-172-4 (cloth : alk. paper)
    1. Brooklyn Bridge (New York, N.Y.) Pictorial works. 2. Suspension
bridges—New York (State)—New York—Maintenance and repair Pictorial
works. 3. Photography, Artistic. I. Lopate, Phillip, 1943–   . II. Title.
TG25.N53D64  1999
779'.47471—dc21                                          99-16548
                                                              CIP

TO ANGELA

# CONTENTS

# INTRODUCTION

BY PHILLIP LOPATE

Confronting the world's most recognizable, reproduced monuments—the Eiffel Tower, the Pyramids, the Acropolis, the Colosseum, the Brooklyn Bridge—the mind tends to go numb. So much devotion has been lavished on these by-now primal shapes that they seem hardwired into our imaginations, iconically omnipresent and therefore refractory to awe. Still, we long to feel the same shiver our ancestors did; and sometimes we have what approximates a religious experience in their proximity, either because of or despite the programming we've received. The rest of the time we must scrape away apathy and make a conscious effort to rekindle our wonderment, by exploring the historical ground against which they first stood out as miraculous.

Of all the world's grand monuments, the oddest, I would think, is the Brooklyn Bridge, because it is so purely functional. This paradox was articulated by America's first important architectural critic, Montgomery Schuyler, when he wrote in 1883, the year it opened: "It so happens that the work which is likely to be our most durable monument, and to convey some knowledge of us to the most remote posterity, is a work of bare utility; not a shrine, not a fortress, not a palace, but a bridge."

"The Eighth Wonder of the World," the Brooklyn Bridge was confidently called at its inauguration; but then, that octal title has been so promiscuously bestowed on so many novelties, long since forgotten, it hardly registers anymore. The difference is that the Brooklyn Bridge has remained celebrated and cherished, long after its technological achievements have been superseded. A skeptic might wonder: Why *is* it still so famous? It was not the first successful suspension bridge in America; it is no longer the longest, or (heretical thought) even the loveliest, even in the greater New York City area. Many modernists would agree with Le Corbusier's 1947 assessment: "The George Washington Bridge over the Hudson is the most beautiful bridge in the world. Made of cables and steel beams, it gleams in the sky like a reversed arch. It is blessed." Yet one would be hard-pressed to picture the George Washington Bridge receiving the sort of lavish fireworks on its hundredth birthday that the Brooklyn Bridge got on its centenary in May 1983. Why has the Brooklyn span remained so alive in the popular culture—witness, as just one example, the enduring jokes about selling it to yokels—while garnering so many high-quality tributes from poets and painters and photographers over the years?

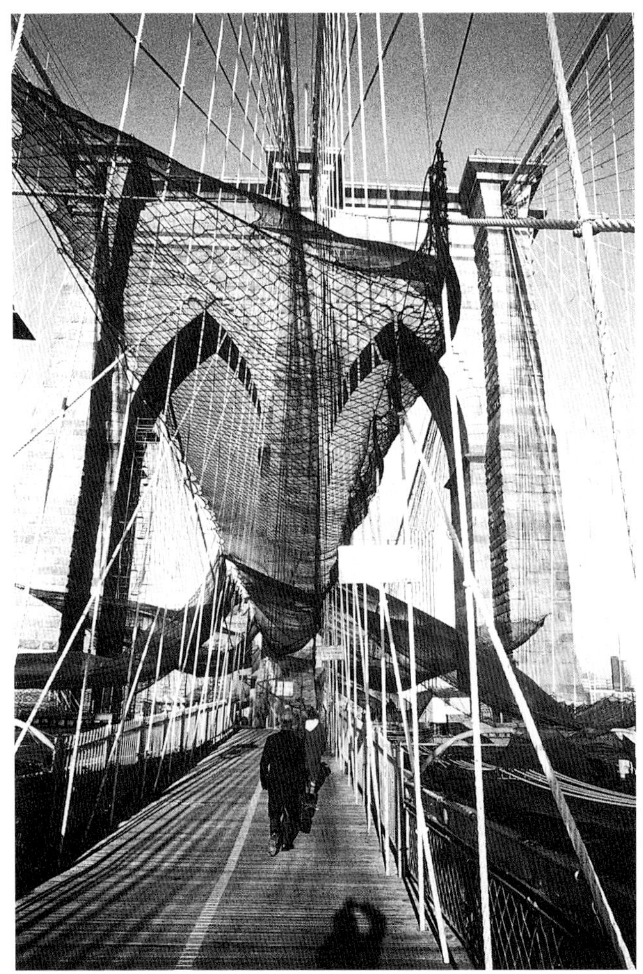

The simplest answer is that it has had the capacity to make itself lovable. Now, beautiful it may also be, but "lovable" is a different quality from "beautiful"; it suggests the knack of inspiring tenderness. If the Brooklyn Bridge began as a magisterial, solitary Alpine range connecting the two great cities of Manhattan and Brooklyn, it soon enough had company across the East River: the Williamsburg Bridge opened in 1903, the Manhattan Bridge in 1905. These siblings forever gamboling at their elder brother's side, elbowing their raw profiles into the view, meant that the Brooklyn Bridge had to be singled out by devotees for something other than its riparian-spanning properties. Here, aesthetics, history, and tradition all came to the rescue.

First, aesthetics: The Brooklyn Bridge is, without a doubt, soaringly, stubbornly beautiful. There is the elegance of the catenary curve (the natural form taken by any rope or cable suspended from two points) as it swoops down to the center and then scallops upward toward the towers; the visual cross-hatching of vertical cables and diagonal stays yielding an effect that has been compared to a harp, a spider's web, angels' wings; the unearthly collision of materials: the airy steel wire of the cables and stays—it was the first bridge to rely solely on steel for such purposes—against the staunch granite towers. Its towers seemed, at the time it was built, the one opportunity to make a consciously monumental statement. In an architecturally eclectic period, faced with the option of borrowing

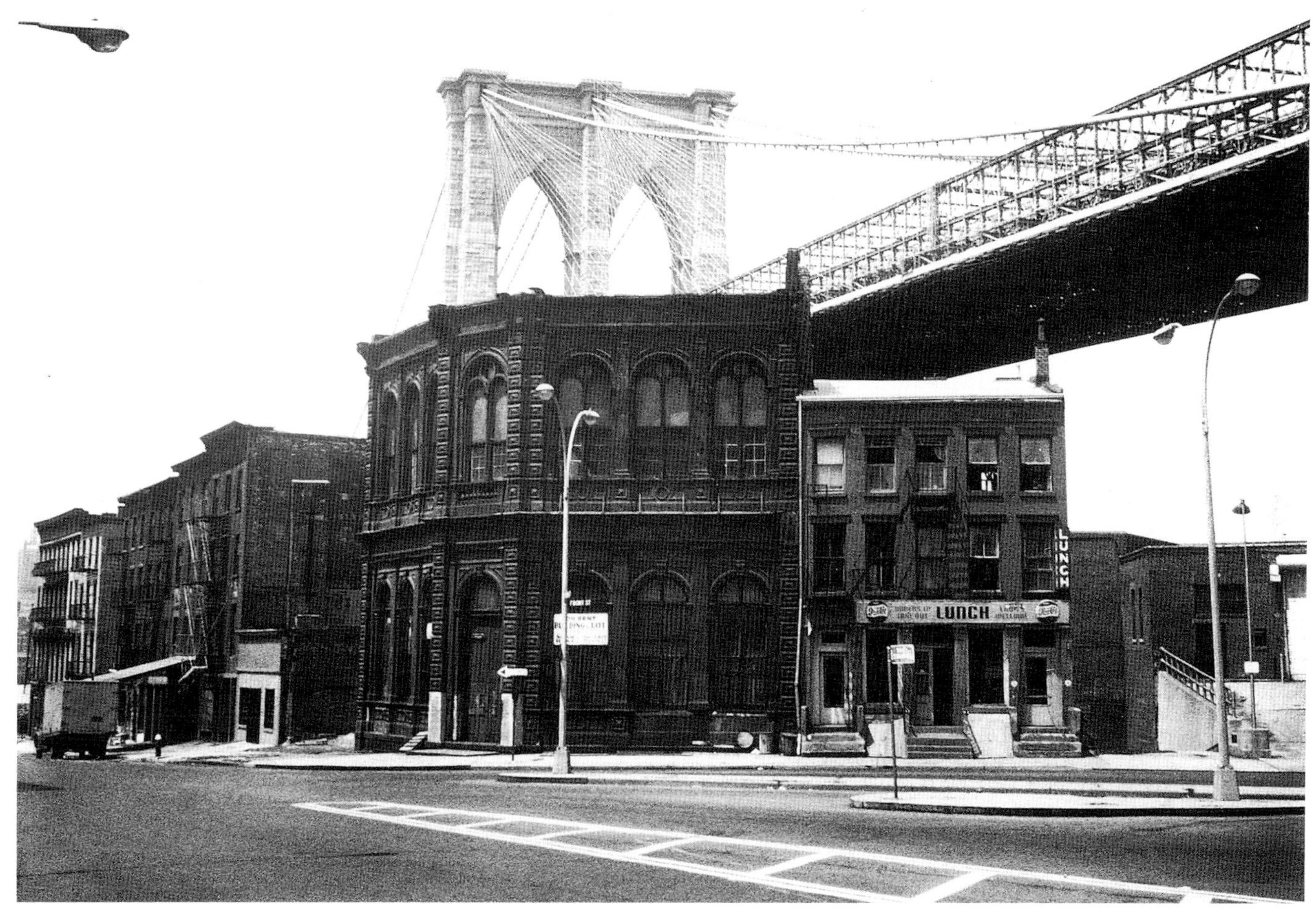

from any historical style (neoclassical, Gothic, French Renaissance), Gothic was chosen for the gateways to the two cities. It was this very dissonance of sleek steel and old-fashioned granite that annoyed Montgomery Schuyler, in his early, proto-modernist assessment, "The Brooklyn Bridge as Monument." After acknowledging that the bridge was perhaps the finest, most enduring structure of the day, Schuyler took issue with the anachronistic heaviness of the Gothic stylings, wishing instead that the towers could have better "revealed" structurally the cables they contained within. It was as though he had in mind a pure steel structure, such as the George Washington Bridge, which is indeed more harmonious, from a modernist aesthetic. But the Brooklyn Bridge is more endearing—more lovable—precisely because it exemplifies that tension, held in stately balance, between old and new, handmade and industrial, granite and gossamer.

Adding to its endearment are the heroic legends about the fourteen-year construction, which still cling to its girders. That Iliadic tale of the struggle to build the Brooklyn Bridge has been told many times, most definitively in David McCullough's fine book *The Great Bridge* (1972): how the stern, brilliant German immigrant-engineer John Augustus Roebling, ex-student of Hegel, having successfully solved the riddle of making suspension bridges safe (maximum stiffness), was offered the assignment to span the East River; how he became its first victim, his

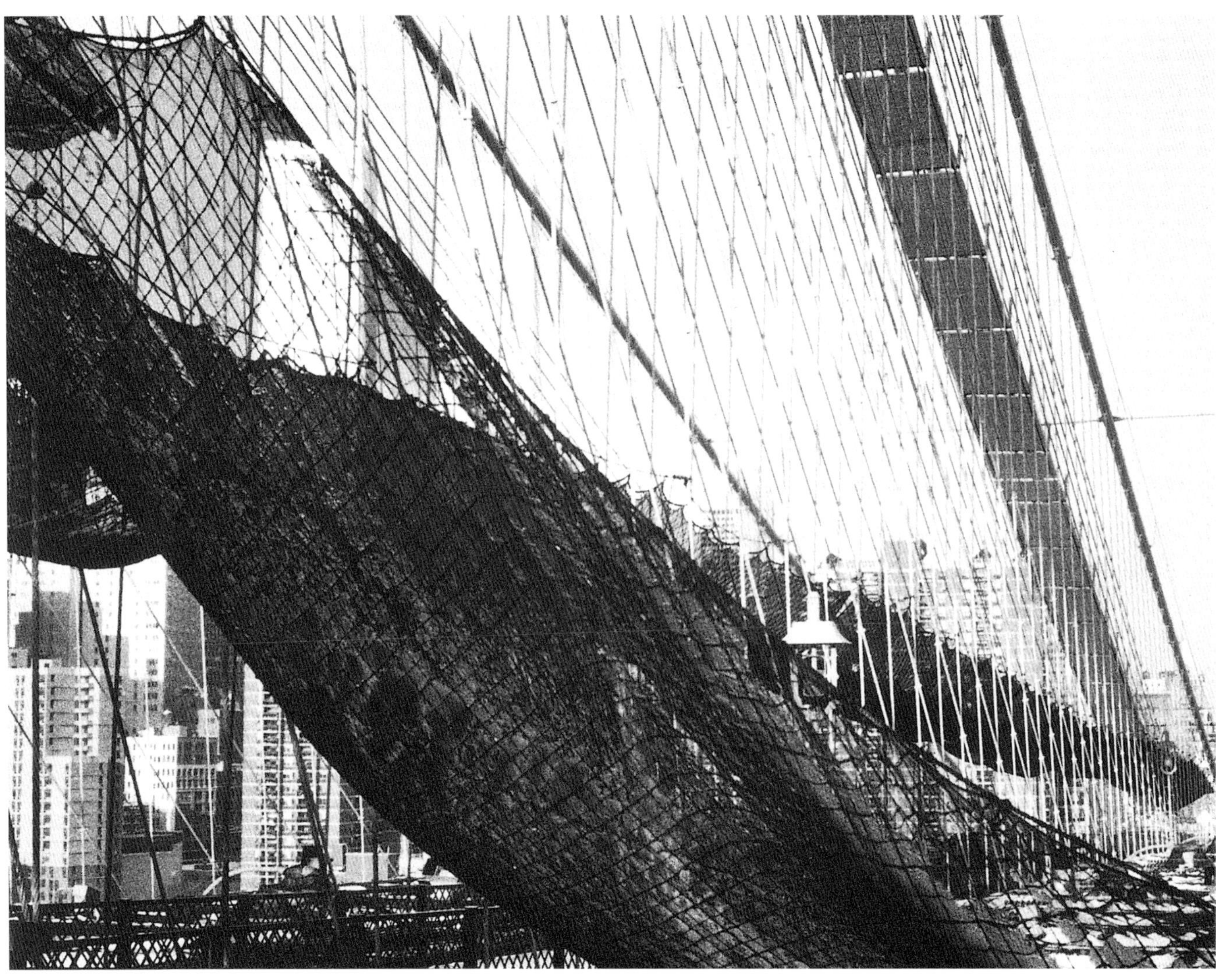

toes crushed by a ferry as he surveyed the tower site, leading to tetanus and death; how his son, Washington, he of calm integrity and superhuman persistence, took over the task, assembled a loyal project team (mostly fellow alumni from the Rensselaer Polytechnic Institute), and set about resourcefully meeting each of the challenges with technological inventions; how they battled the elements and turbulent tides and geological surprises of the East River; how they built two enormous compressed-air foundations, or caissons, each weighing six million pounds, and sunk them underwater to dredge and anchor the towers; how the laborers, working eight-hour shifts with primitive equipment (no power tools!) in these ill-lit, poorly ventilated, sweltering underwater conditions for two dollars a day, began suffering from caisson sickness, or "the bends," which crippled them; how their boss, Washington Roebling, investigating a fire in the caisson, himself contracted the disease and became an invalid for life, forced to attend the bridge's construction from his bedroom window with a spyglass; how he developed, along with the physical disease, a nervous disorder—a neurotically unsociable manner close to misanthropy; how his devoted wife, Emily, played the "bridge" with his associates and employers, smoothing over public demands for her husband's resignation as chief engineer; how the gluttonous William Macy Tweed, ruler of Tammany Hall, saw this massive public works project as a splendid opportunity for graft and almost took it, but the Tweed Ring was exposed and busted in the nick of time; how a corrupt supplier of steel wire, a bigamist mountebank who gained the contract through political kickbacks, managed to smuggle in substandard materials, despite Roebling's orders that every yard of wire be personally inspected; how it didn't matter, finally, because Roebling had already factored in that the bridge be built six times its necessary strength; how it mattered only symbolically, in that there would always be invisible weaknesses woven into the bridge's near-perfection, just as blood was admixed into its joints and bolts from the deaths of some twenty workmen.

As Alan Trachtenberg pointed out in his excellent study, *Brooklyn Bridge: Fact and Symbol* (1965): "For many Americans in 1883, Brooklyn Bridge proved the nation to be healed of its wounds of civil war and again on its true course: the peaceful mastery of nature." It was the age of engineer-heroes (Ferdinand de Lesseps, Roebling) and engineering feats, and nothing stirred the public's romantic sentiment more than bridges: "Babylon had her hanging garden, Egypt her pyramid, Athens her Acropolis, Rome her Atheneum; so Brooklyn has her Bridge," boasted a shopkeeper's sign on the holiday of its opening. The bridge had been strung with lightbulbs, making it the first electrified span over water. But such innovations, again, are easily forgotten: What kept the Brooklyn Bridge alive in the minds of people was its significance in the mythos and daily life of New York City. The bridge unified two great cities as physically as a rope tied around their waists: It had been designed in such a way as to connect New York's city hall with the city hall of Brooklyn; to extend, as it were, Broadway to Fulton Street. The success of the bridge preempted charter revision: It made the amalgamation of the five boroughs a few years later, in 1898, into one super-metropolis, a kind of inevitability, an afterthought.

"I hereby prophecy that in 1900 A.D. Brooklyn will be the city and New York will be the suburb," wrote George Templeton Strong in his diary in 1865. "It is inevitable if both go on growing as they have grown for the last forty years. Brooklyn has room to spread and New York has not." Brooklyn was the coming place; no one anticipated that Manhattan would grow vertically. It was Brooklyn, then the fifth-largest city in the nation, that had agitated most for the bridge, thinking correctly that it would drive up the value of its Heights real estate and attract middle-class businessmen by making their commute easier than the unreliable, ice-bound ferries. It was Brooklyn that had supplied the vast majority of planning and political energies for the building of the bridge, and paid the lion's share of the construction costs. So it was only fair that what had been originally called "the East River Bridge" would undergo a name change to honor its sponsoring agent. The irony is that the bridge both put Brooklyn on the map and diminished it forever, by undermining its urban independence. However much the residents of Kings County might cling to their faith that Brooklyn was still the emerging urban hub, its destiny was to be a provincial, if eccentric, bedroom borough to Manhattan.

For Manhattanites the bridge became, as David McCullough put it, "a highway into the open air." One of Roebling's great design decisions had been to build an elevated promenade, which would arch ever so slightly, so as to bow *above* the traffic. The walker would have the freedom of the city: to look down at vehicles crossing the bridge (first, horse-drawn carriages and elevated trains; later, cars), or else to ignore them and gaze uninterruptedly in every direction, at the water, the boats (innumerable, during the East River's heyday as a port), the skyline, and the sky itself.

From where else can one see the whole city today? From skyscraper observatories, certainly, such as the Empire State Building or the World Trade Center, but one has to pay a fee, and then, once aloft, the pacing possibilities have distinct limits; whereas the Brooklyn Bridge promenade is an extension of the street system, a great free thoroughfare, a flaneur's arena for strolling, dawdling, or even romancing.

Governor Al Smith, in his autobiography, *Up to Now* (1929), fondly recalled: "In its early days the bridge served as more than a utility for transportation between the two cities. It soon became a place of recreation and of pleasure. So much so that it was referred to in songs and popularized on the variety stage. I can still sing 'Danny by my side':

> The Brooklyn Bridge on Sunday is known as lover's lane,
> I stroll there with my sweetheart, oh, time and time again;
> Oh, how I love to ramble, oh, yes, it is my pride,
> Dressed in my best, each day of rest, with Danny by my side.

The lordly position of the pedestrian on the promenade must have suited Washington Roebling, who refused to enter a motorcar in his lifetime. (He died in 1926.) On the other hand, there is irony in the fact that this superb public space was built by a man who, after his bout with caisson sickness, hated to be in crowds and found it a torment to socialize with anyone but his wife for more than a few minutes.

The bridge was also inspiration to poets and loners. The experience recounted by the critic Lewis Mumford in his autobiography, *Sketches from Life* (1981), is archetypical of many lyrical literary responses the Brooklyn Bridge evoked. On a March day, the then-youthful Mumford was walking into Manhattan at twilight, and

> as I reached the middle of the Brooklyn Bridge, the sunlight spread across the sky, forming a halo around the jagged mountain of skyscrapers, with the darkened loft buildings and warehouses huddling below in the foreground. The towers, topped by the golden pinnacles of the new Woolworth Building, still caught the light even as it began to ebb away. Three-quarters of the way across the Bridge I saw the skyscrapers in the deepening darkness become slowly honeycombed with lights until, before I reached the Manhattan end, these buildings piled up in a dazzling mass against the indigo sky.
>
> Here was my city, immense, overpowering, flooded with energy and light.... And there was I, breasting the March wind, drinking in the city and the sky, both vast, yet both contained in me, transmitting through me the great mysterious will that had made them and the promise of the new day that was still to come.

Mumford, looking backward half a century, remembers being filled with an exaltation that he compares to "the wonder of an orgasm in the body of one's beloved." He writes: "In that sudden revelation of power and beauty all the confusions of adolescence dropped from me, and I trod the narrow, resilient boards of the footway with a new confidence that came, not from my isolated self alone but from the collective energies I had confronted and risen to."

Here the Brooklyn Bridge is a cradle for self-creation as well as ecstasy. Like Rastignac in Balzac's *Père Goriot*, waving his fist at Paris below and swearing he will conquer it someday, Mumford vows to extract the fullest from his talents and to affect the city stretched tantalizingly around him. The elevated, 360-degree vantage point offered by the bridge inspires feelings of wholeness bordering on omnipotence.

It was inevitable that the Russian poet Vladimir Mayakovsky, so charmingly susceptible to grandiosity, should find a ready subject for contemplation in the celebrated structure, which he visited in 1925. In his poem "Brooklyn Bridge," he compares himself to a "conqueror" who steps with pride onto its back.

I am proud
        of just this
                mile of steel;
upon it,
        my visions come to life, erect—
here's a fight
            for construction
                    instead of style,
an austere disposition
                of bolts
                        and steel.
If
    the end of the world
                befall—
and chaos
        smash our planet
                to bits,
and what remains
            will be
                this
bridge, rearing above the dust of destruction;
then,
        as huge ancient lizards
                are rebuilt
from bones
        finer than needles,
                to tower in museums
so,
    from this bridge,

                    a geologist of the centuries
          will succeed
                in recreating
                        our contemporary world.

Mayakovsky yokes social-realist imagery to prehistoric musings. So now the Brooklyn Bridge has become something like a dinosaur, whose bones alone will survive the apocalypse of the twentieth century.

The idea of the Brooklyn Bridge as an enormous machine is not original with Mayakovsky: It was first proposed by another visitor, Henry James, who, returning to his native city after twenty years abroad, recorded with something like horror, in his travel book *The American Scene,* his reaction to the span. "This appearance of the bold lacing together, across the waters, of the scattered members of the monstrous organism," begins one of those tortuous late-Jamesian sentences, during which he compares the bridge to a steam engine and a power loom, before returning to his Frankenstein's monster metaphor:

> One has the sense that the monster grows and grows, flinging aboard its loose limbs even as some unmannered young giant at his "larks," and that the binding stitches must forever fly further and faster and draw harder; the future complexity of the web, all under sky and above the sea, becoming thus that of some colossal set of clockworks, some steel-souled machine-room of brandished arms and hammering fists and opening and closing jaws.

For James, writing in 1907, the Brooklyn Bridge was still too new—too suggestive of the ominous threat of industrialized conformity—to be cherished as a work of local genius. But Hart Crane saw and understood the lonely grandeur and achievement of the bridge from a more sympathetic, historically removed perspective. He had researched the Roeblings with an eye toward writing their biography. To inhabit their inner world more, he even rented the same apartment on Hicks Street, in Brooklyn Heights, that Washington Roebling had occupied while overseeing the bridge's construction. "Brooklyn Bridge," wrote Crane in a letter to his family, is "the most superb piece of construction in the modern world, I'm sure, with strings of lights crossing it like glowing worms as the Ls and surface cars pass each other coming and going." He chose it as his symbol of affirmation in *The Bridge* (1930), his American response to T. S. Eliot's *The Waste Land* (1922). Among its many gorgeous, exhilarating lines are these that end the prologue, addressed directly "To Brooklyn Bridge":

> O harp and altar, of the fury fused,
> (How could mere toil align thy choiring strings!)
> Terrific threshold of the prophet's pledge,
> Prayer of pariah, and the lover's cry,—

Again the traffic lights that skim thy swift
Unfractioned idiom, immaculate sigh of stars,
Beading thy path—condense eternity:
And we have seen night lifted in thine arms.

Under thy shadow by the piers I waited;
Only in darkness is thy shadow clear.
The City's fiery parcels all undone,
Already snow submerges an iron year…

O sleepless as the river under thee,
Vaulting the sea, the prairies' dreaming sod,
Unto us lowliest sometime sweep, descend
And of the curveship lend a myth to God.

Crane encircles the bridge with spiritual connotations: A "curveship," like an alien spaceship dropped down from the galaxies, it redeems the prophet's pledge, sets up heavenly choirs, lifts night in its arms, condenses eternity, and to top it all, lends its own myth to a God who seems, in our secular age, in need of one.

It is interesting that so many of the most memorable paeans to the Brooklyn Bridge, in poetry (Crane, Mayakovsky, Garcia Lorca), prose (John Dos Passos, Thomas Wolfe, Henry Miller), and paint (Joseph Stella, John Marin, Albert Gleizes, Marsden Hartley), were fashioned from just after the First World War through the 1920s and 1930s, when the structure had already been standing for a number of decades. It no longer was a technological novelty, but its glamour had, if anything, skyrocketed. Why this was the case may have as much to do with the development of modernism—American modernism in particular—as with any singularities of the Brooklyn Bridge.

In his essay collection *Port of New York* (1924), the critic Paul Rosenfeld wrote about fourteen American moderns, who included Arthur Dove, John Marin, William Carlos Williams, Alfred Stieglitz, Georgia O'Keeffe, and Marsden Hartley. He analyzed what he called "the drama of cultural awakening" in the America of the 1920s, using the Port of New York as a central, organizing image. No longer was it necessary for bohemians and artists to go abroad, Rosenfeld argued: "For what we once could feel only by quitting New York—the fundamental oneness we have with the place and the people in it—that is sensible to us today in the very jostling, abstracted streets of the city. We know it here, our relationship with this place in which we live. The buildings cannot deprive us of it. For they and we have suddenly commenced growing together." If the buildings were entwining their roots into the artists' souls, how much more so their beloved bridge, the mother of local modernism, which spanned the very same crucial Port of New York.

$S$uch fervent, mythifying worship could not continue at the same heat. It was too much to put on any bridge, however awesomely endearing. The literary tributes began to fall away, though Roebling's eighth wonder continued to be the most photographed bridge in the world. If most of these photographs were tourist snapshots or postcard images, banal in the extreme, all the more so did the bridge challenge the trained professional. How to avoid the clichés? Should one attempt to grasp the whole sweep of it, or capture its essence through intense fragments? How much of the surrounding city ought to enter the composition? Should one flatten the depth of field, collapse foreground into background (as Joseph Stella did in his semi-Cubist painted renderings), or emphasize the separation of visual planes? Where to situate oneself in order to take the best image? Above, below, to the side? How to capture a historical awareness of the bridge: the changes that Time—or our own mutating aesthetic perceptions—had wrought on it?

Burhan Dogançay's photographic series, selected here, forms one of the most sustained and serious artistic responses to the Brooklyn Bridge in our time. The distinguished painter and photographer, born in Turkey in 1929, is best known perhaps for his extraordinary series of wall photographs and graffiti (twenty-five thousand slides from around the world). Dogançay has lived in New York, a city he loves and has explored relentlessly on foot, since 1962. After he arrived, he would take visiting friends to the Brooklyn Bridge and show it off as one of

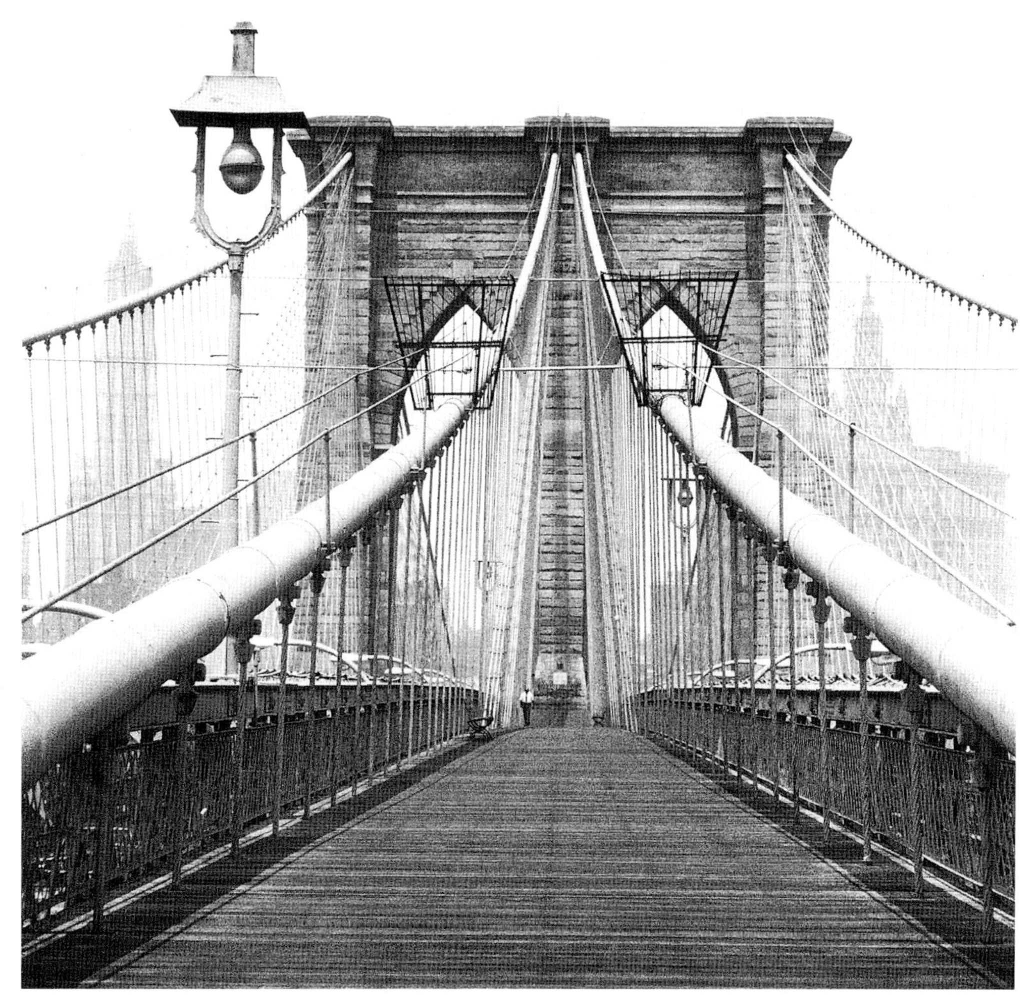

his favorite places in town; he occasionally photographed and painted it as well. But twenty-five years would elapse before he explored the bridge systematically; and his re-approach to this subject followed an indirect and unexpected path.

Essentially, Dogançay, while photographing walls, became fascinated with the ironworkers who put up skyscrapers in Midtown. These daredevils tightrope-walked girders hundreds of feet above the ground, for the most part disdaining safety belts and other attachments. He began photographing, in depth, the crew who were erecting Philip Johnson's "Lipstick Building"; he and the men became friends. (He respected their courage and skill; they, his artistry and willingness to take chances for a difficult shot.) He became the "semi-official artist" of their union, donating several prints to the union hall. When the job was done, they invited him to follow them to three other buildings, and after that, to the Brooklyn Bridge, where they had been assigned to work on a major restoration effort in the late 1980s.

"The first day that I went to shoot pictures of iron workers on the Brooklyn Bridge, I was truly afraid to go to the top," Dogançay says. "I had gotten used to moving around on construction sites in Midtown Manhattan, but being high up over the East River on a freezing, windy day was another matter.

"I went up to a place that was high above the roadway and even higher above the river," he continues. "Down below, cars and boats passed like toys. This was the point where the iron workers had erected a scaffolding with a ladder against the wall of the bridge's arch. Close to the top of the arch I could see the squeeze hole, the entry to a shaft that leads to the parapet." Since the only alternative was climbing along the cables, Dogançay braced himself and managed to squeeze up that narrow shaft, passing, as he did, some graffiti from 1888, one hundred years before. The men applauded his pluck. A stunt, perhaps; but he had proven, to himself at least, that he could photograph the bridge in the hardest conditions.

During the next two years, he took hundreds of photographs of the restoration work. The result is not the tourists' bridge: As the footway often needed to be closed during this repair work, pedestrians rarely figure in the shots. The uniqueness of this record is that the Brooklyn Bridge is covered in safety nets. They appear to double the famous webbing effect of diagonal stays crisscrossed with cable wire. The bridge, like a bride or widow (take your pick), wears a veil over its face. In some of the photographs, the bridge resembles a fishing village, its nets hung out to dry; in others, the columns look like masts on sailing boats. The nets' overall effect is to offer some mediation: a screen between everyday life and another reality that may lie just beyond.

Dogançay's photographs dramatize the tense play of light and shadow in the Brooklyn Bridge's form: the granite arches that loom like minarets, beckoning the traveler to prayer. They draw our attention to the haunting shadow of the bridge on water. They accentuate the serpentine plunge of the railing, like a roller coaster descending into the high-rise city. They retrieve the chiseled historic detail of stonework, the juxtaposition of

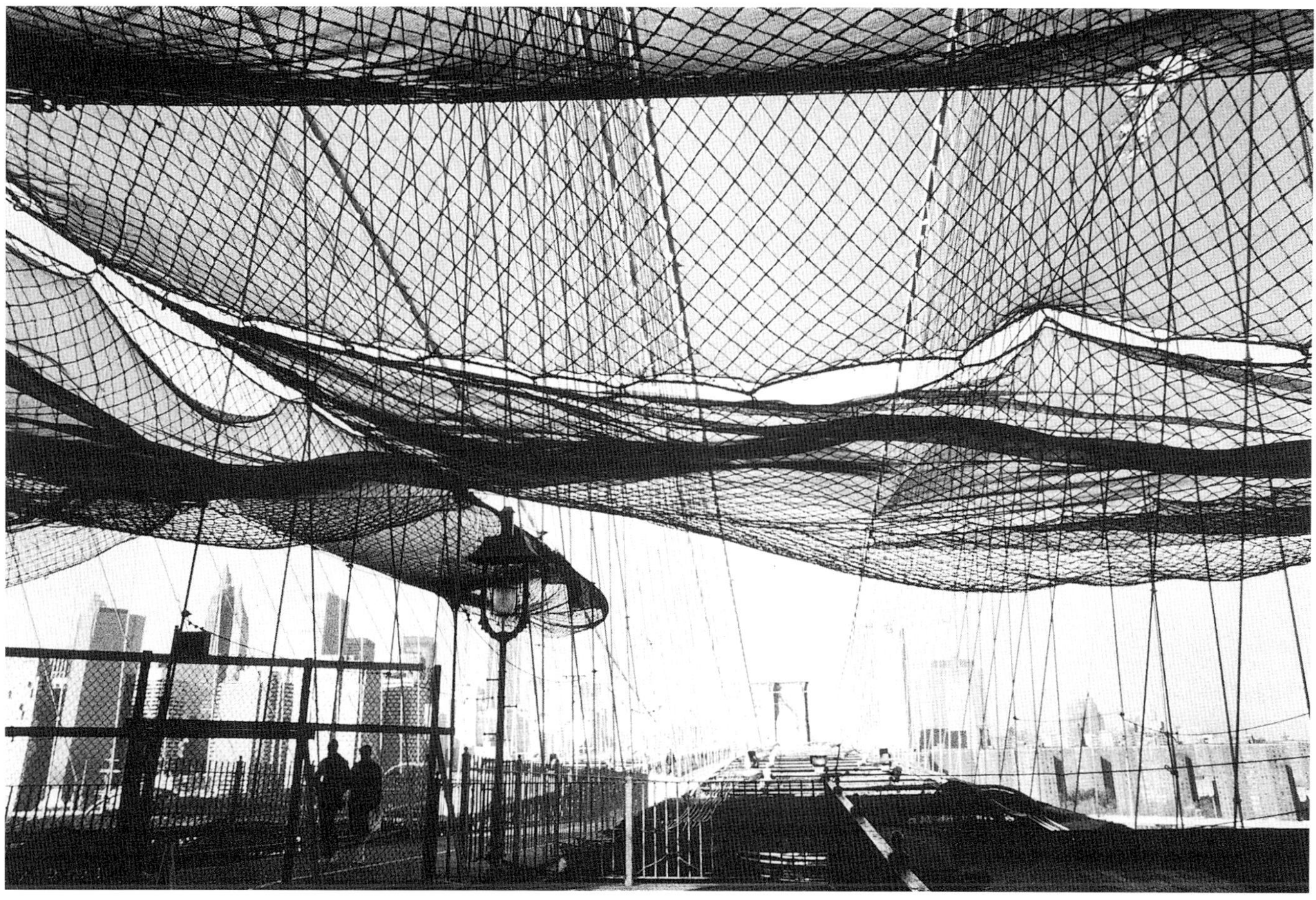

Victorian lamps with postmodern artifacts. They obsess over the relationship between the bridge and the metropolis: on one side, flamboyant, vertical Manhattan; on the other, a more horizontal, vastly spread-out Brooklyn. But most of all, they document the terrifyingly acrobatic intrepidity of the ironworkers, these sky-walkers who function, as the saying goes, without a net. (The nets, incidentally, were installed to protect vehicles and pedestrians, not the repair workers.) How calm they look in their hard hats as they perch over the river, one misstep away from catastrophe; how relaxed, as they drink their coffee through ski masks necessitated by the bitter cold, the fabulous city absorbed into the background.

"When the perfected East River bridge shall permanently and uninterruptedly connect the two cities," the editor of the *Brooklyn Eagle,* Thomas Kinsella, predicted in 1872 with some regret, "the daily thousands who cross it will consider it a sort of natural and inevitable phenomenon, such as the rising and setting of the sun, and they will unconsciously overlook the preliminary difficulties surmounted before the structure spanned the stream, and will perhaps undervalue the indomitable courage, the absolute faith, the consummate genius which assured the engineer's triumph." Dogançay has chosen, in a sense, to go back to the romance of labor, the original big story in the making of the bridge, by focusing on the nineteenth-century workmen's natural descendants, the ironworkers who have restored and protected their endeavor. "How could mere toil align thy choiring strings!" demanded Hart Crane. But apparently, mere toil did—and does. As Dogançay himself puts it: "I thought, What has changed since Egyptian times? In spite of all this progress, they still do everything with their muscles." If these platinum-printed photographs possess an archaic tinge, an aura of melancholy that recalls Alfred Stieglitz and Edward Steichen, as well as Lewis Hine, it may be because they convey an appreciation for the mutual dependency of nature and humanity, of monumental stone and gritty sweat, that is as noble as it is ancient.

# BRIDGE OF DREAMS

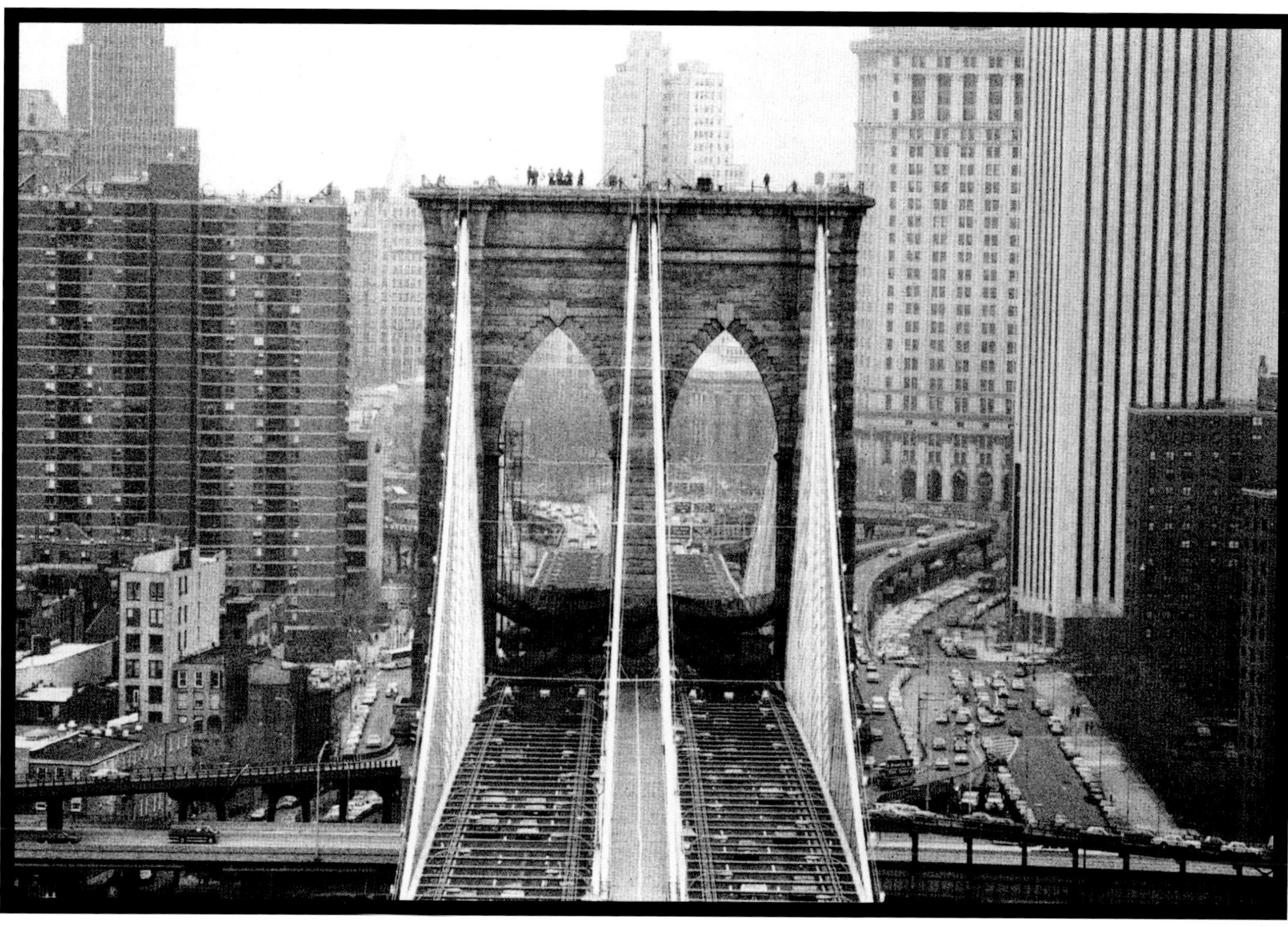

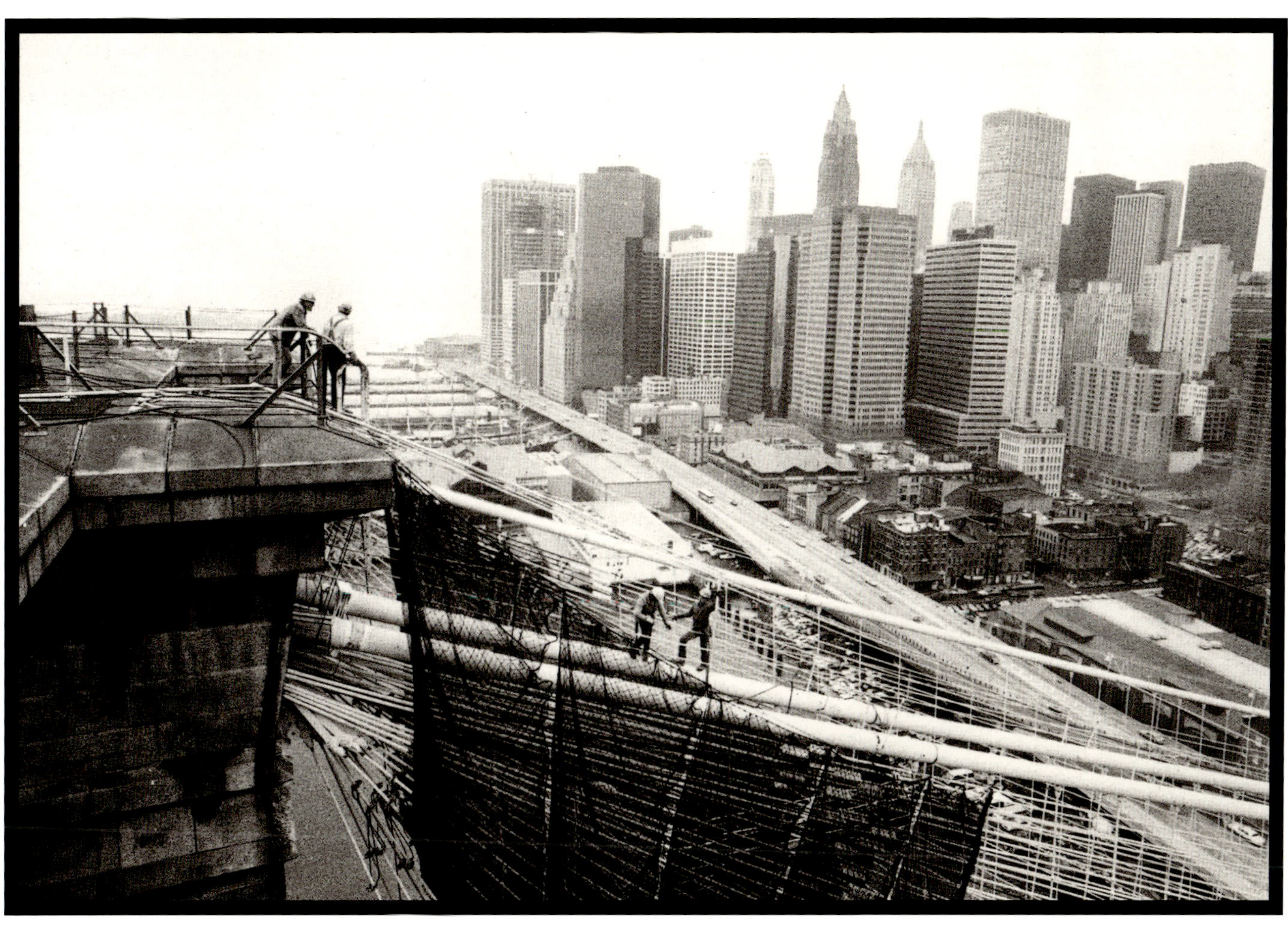

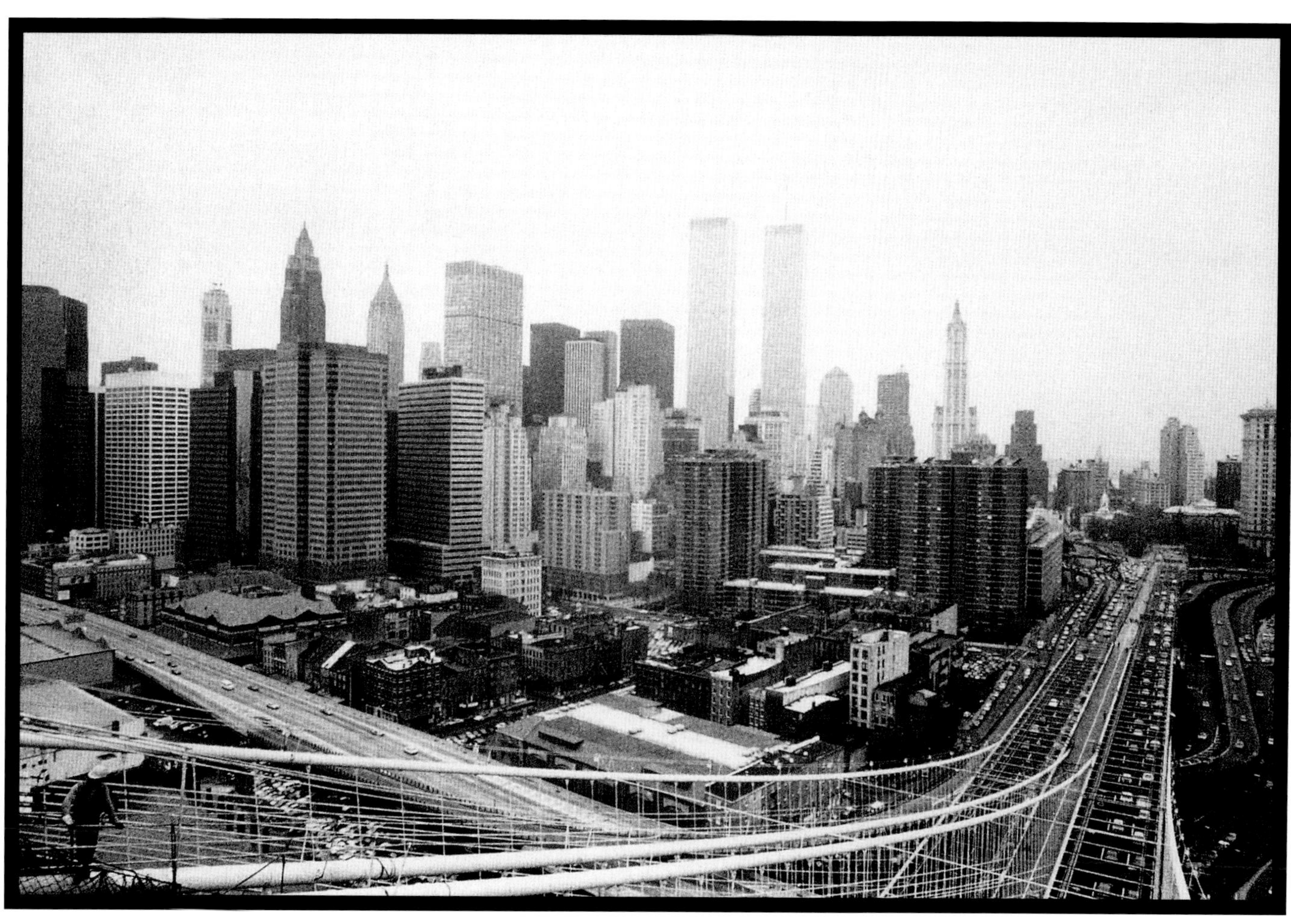

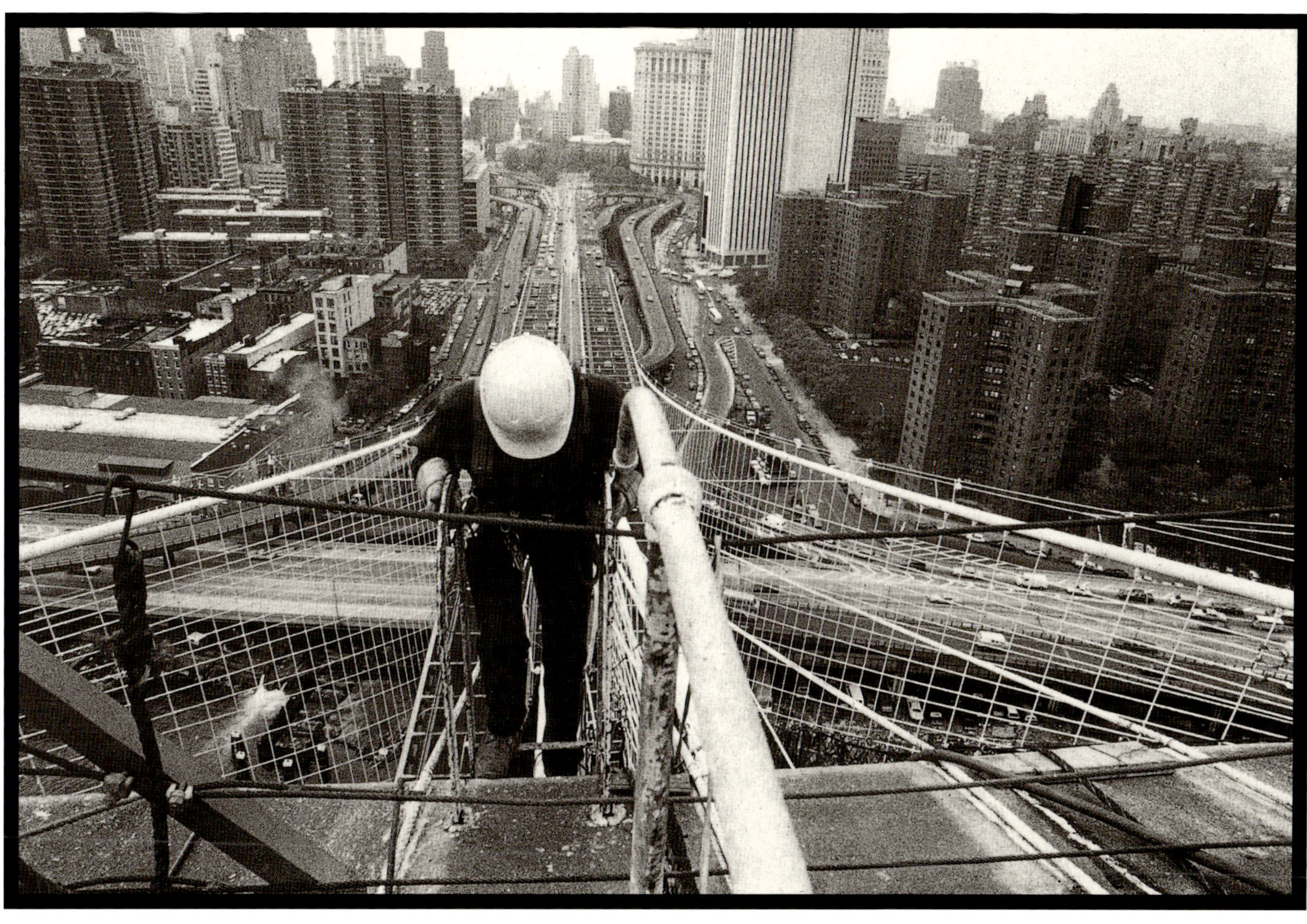

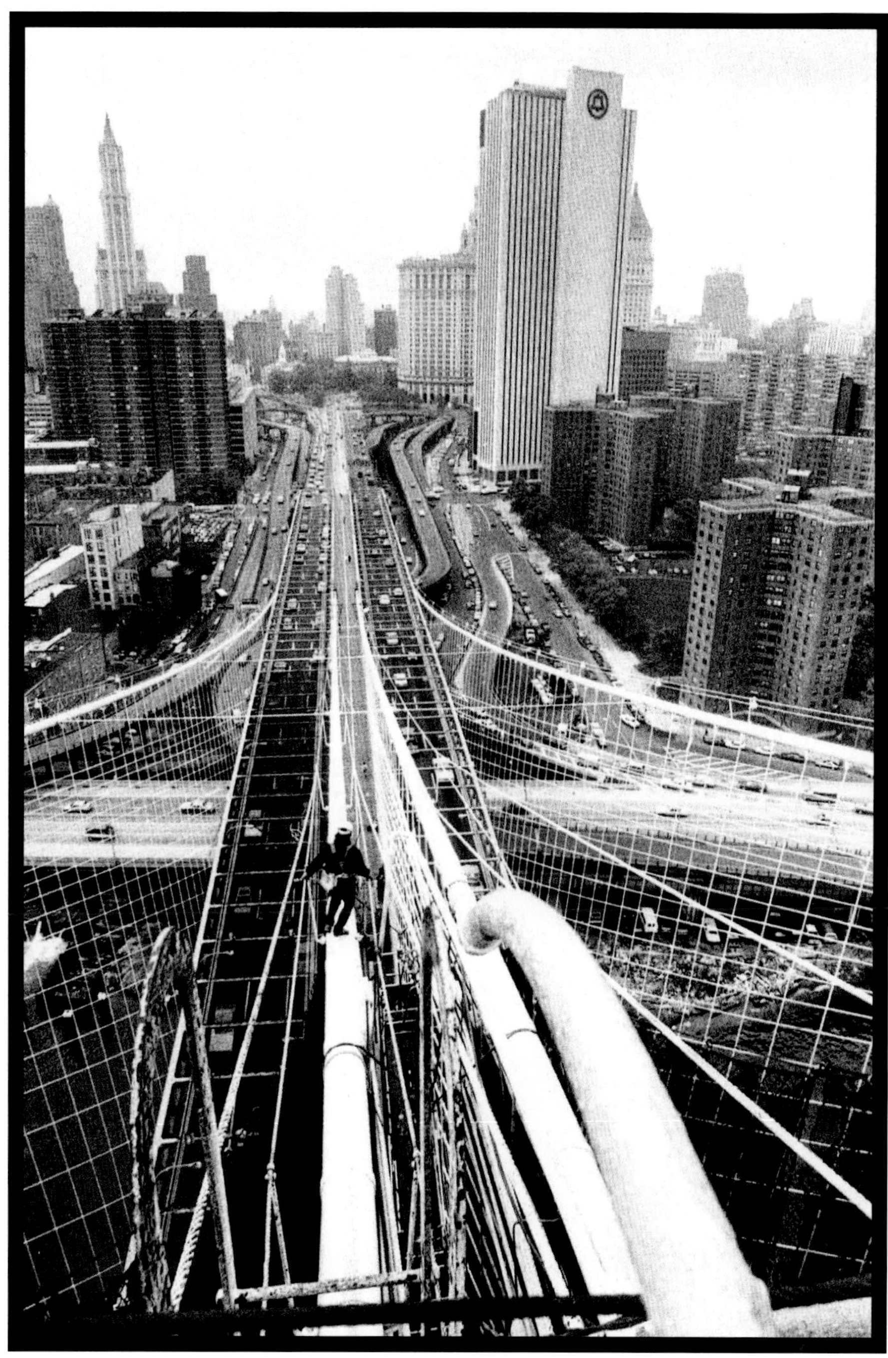

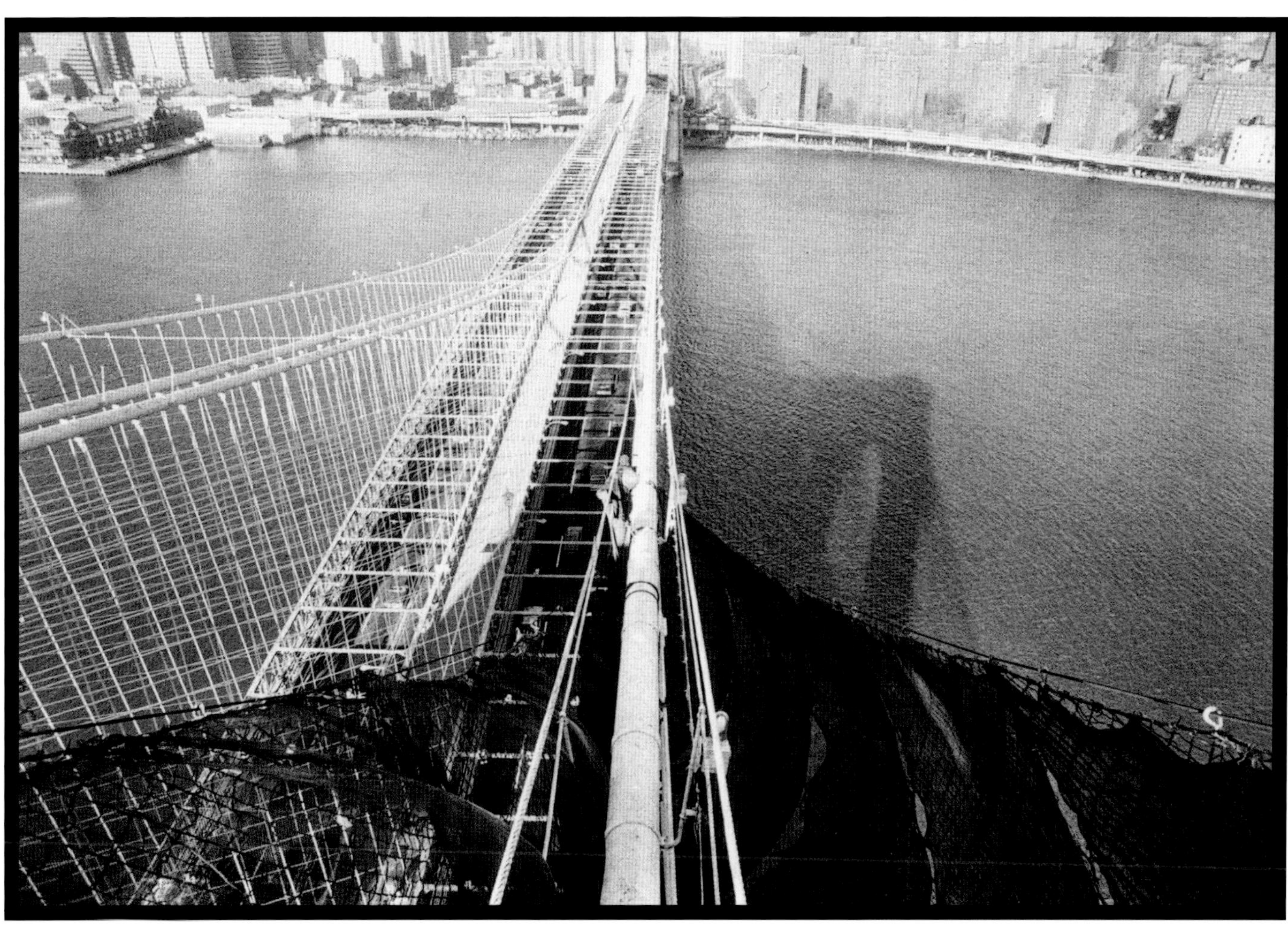

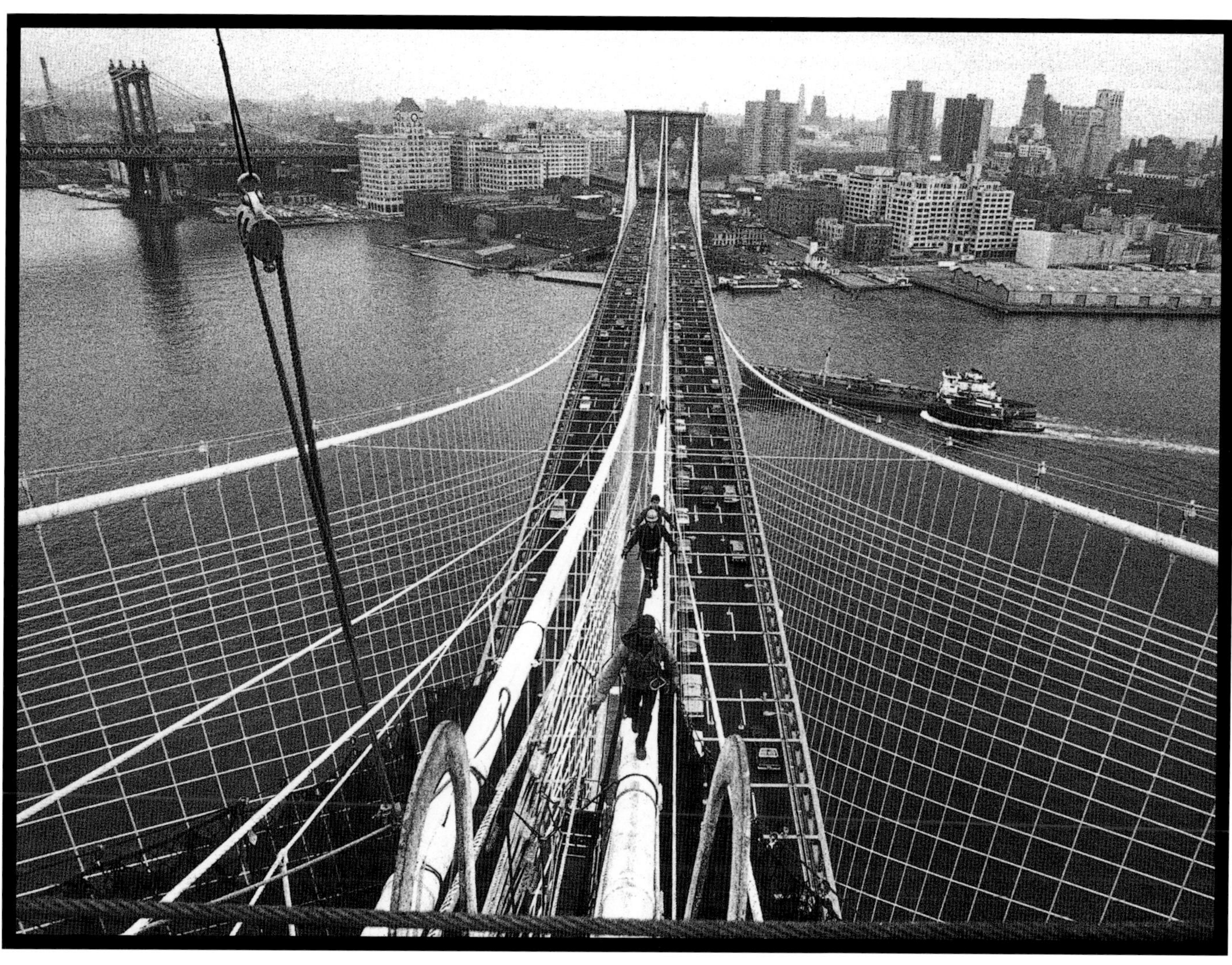

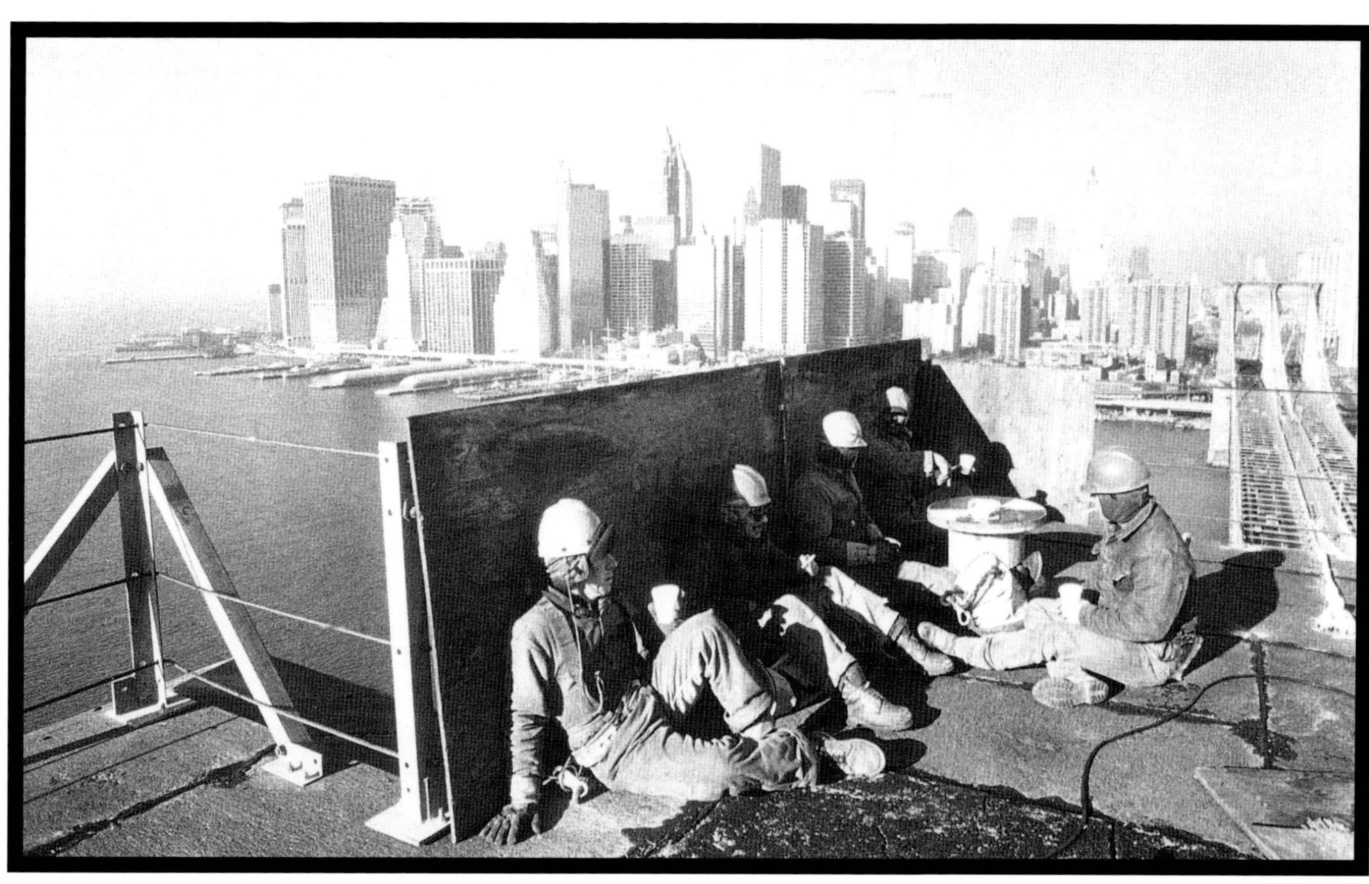

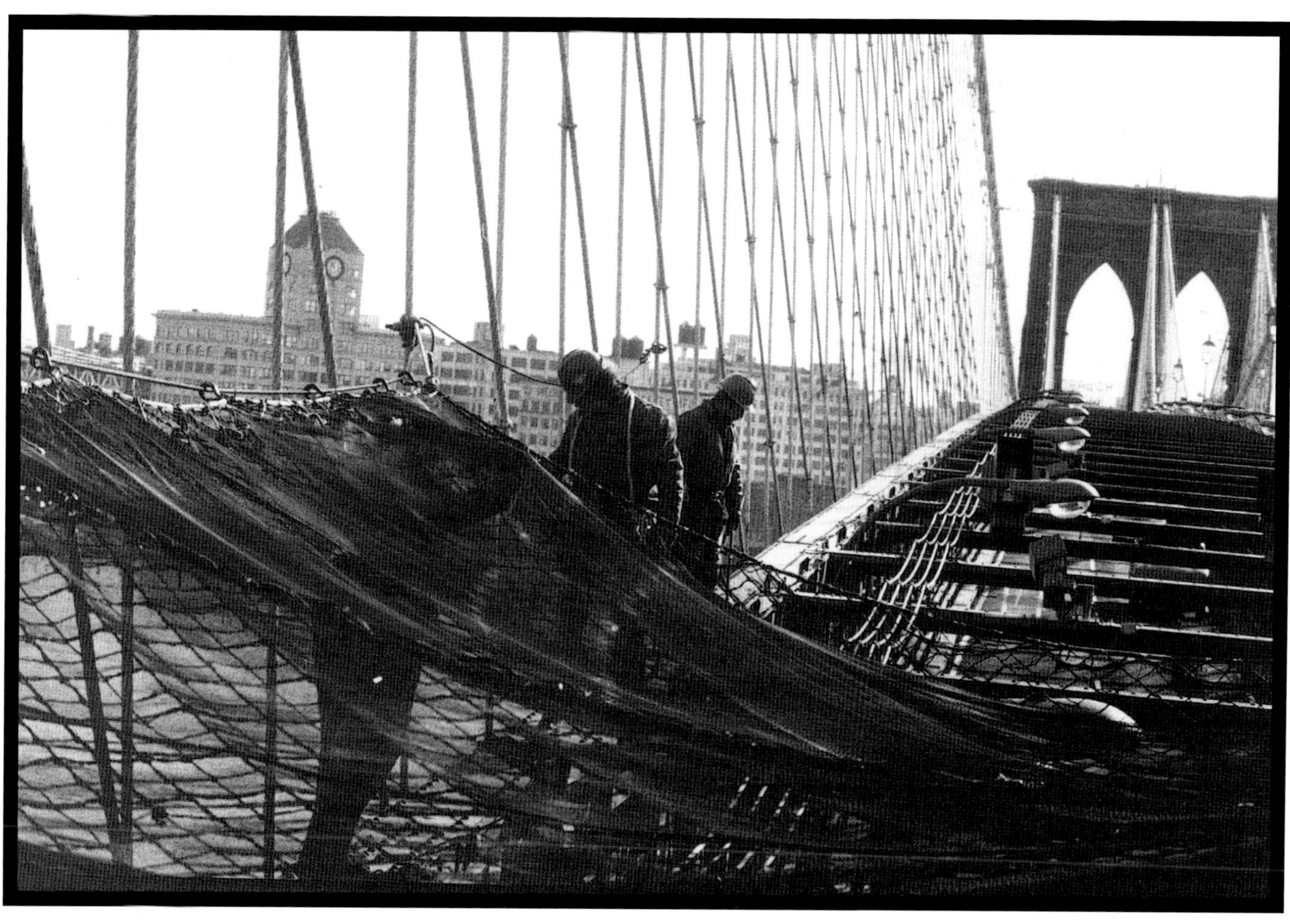

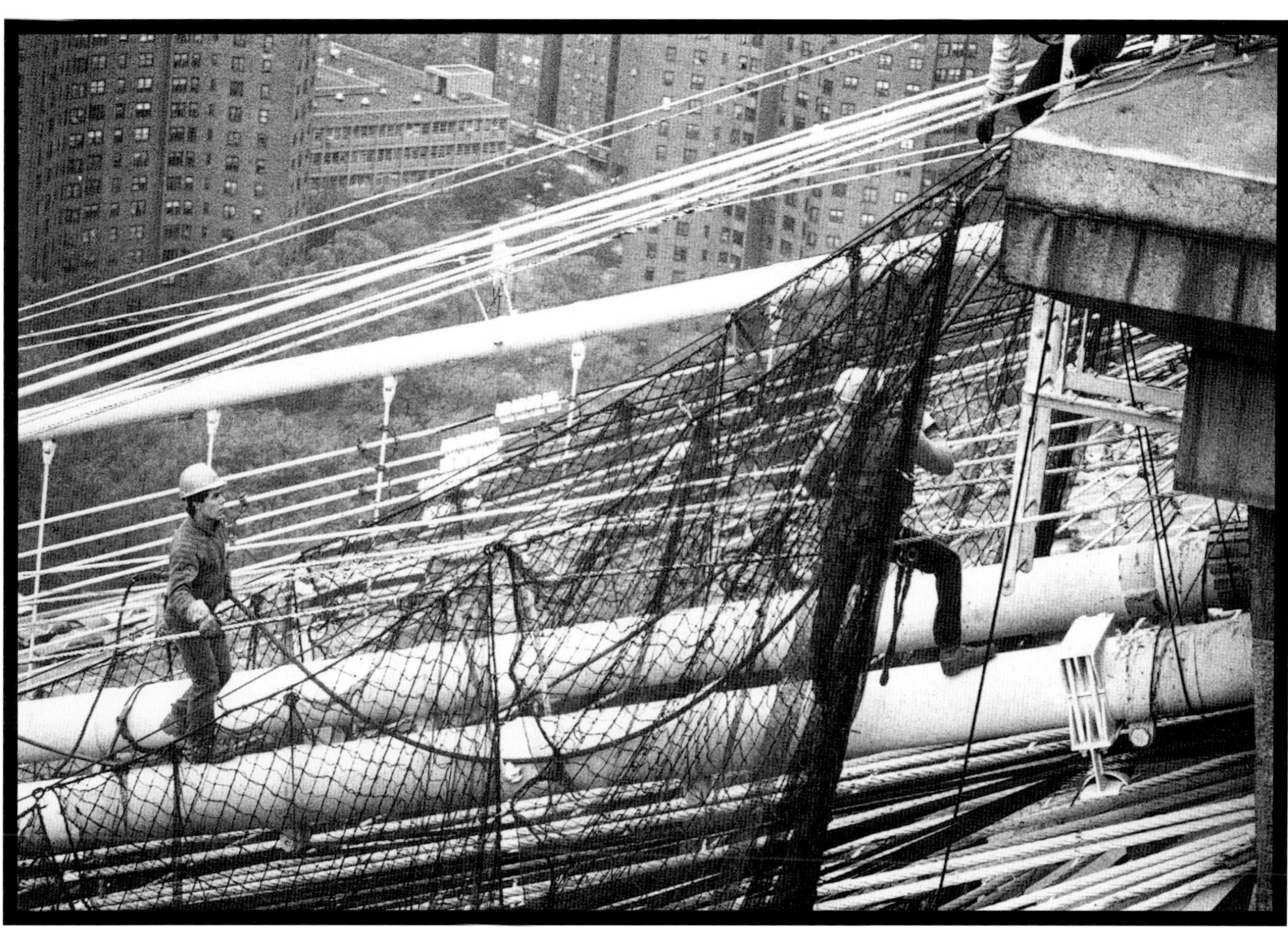

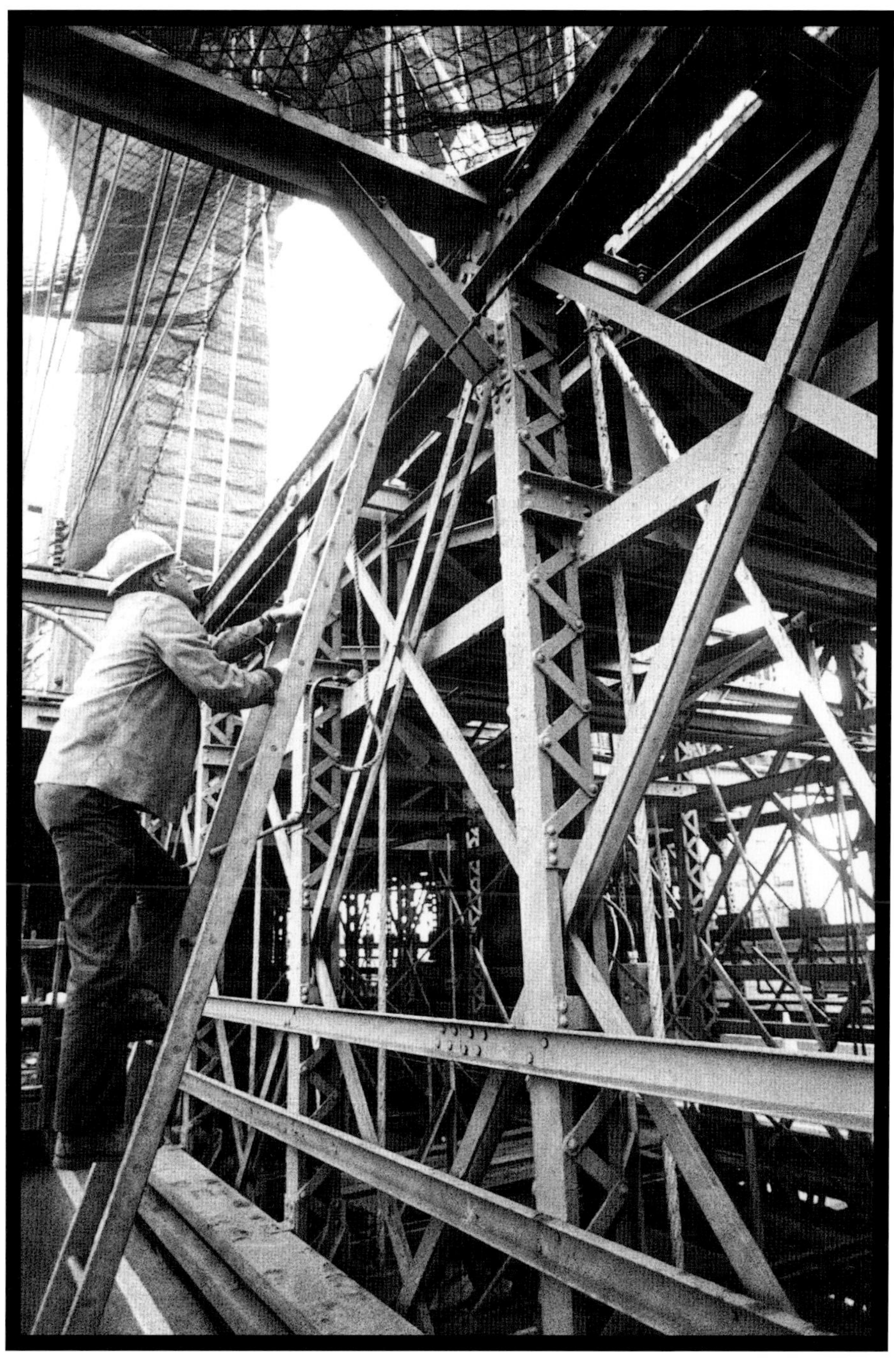

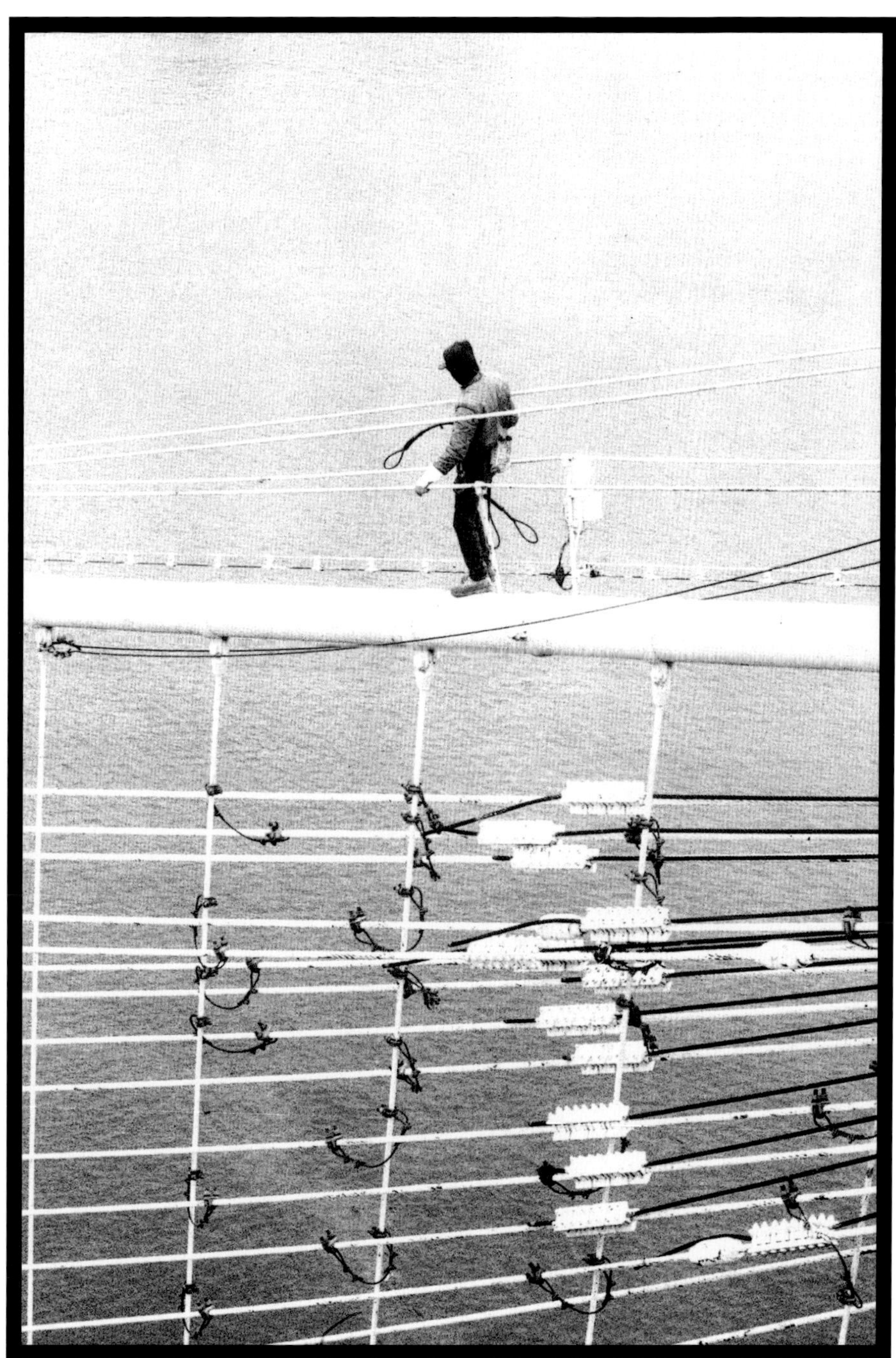

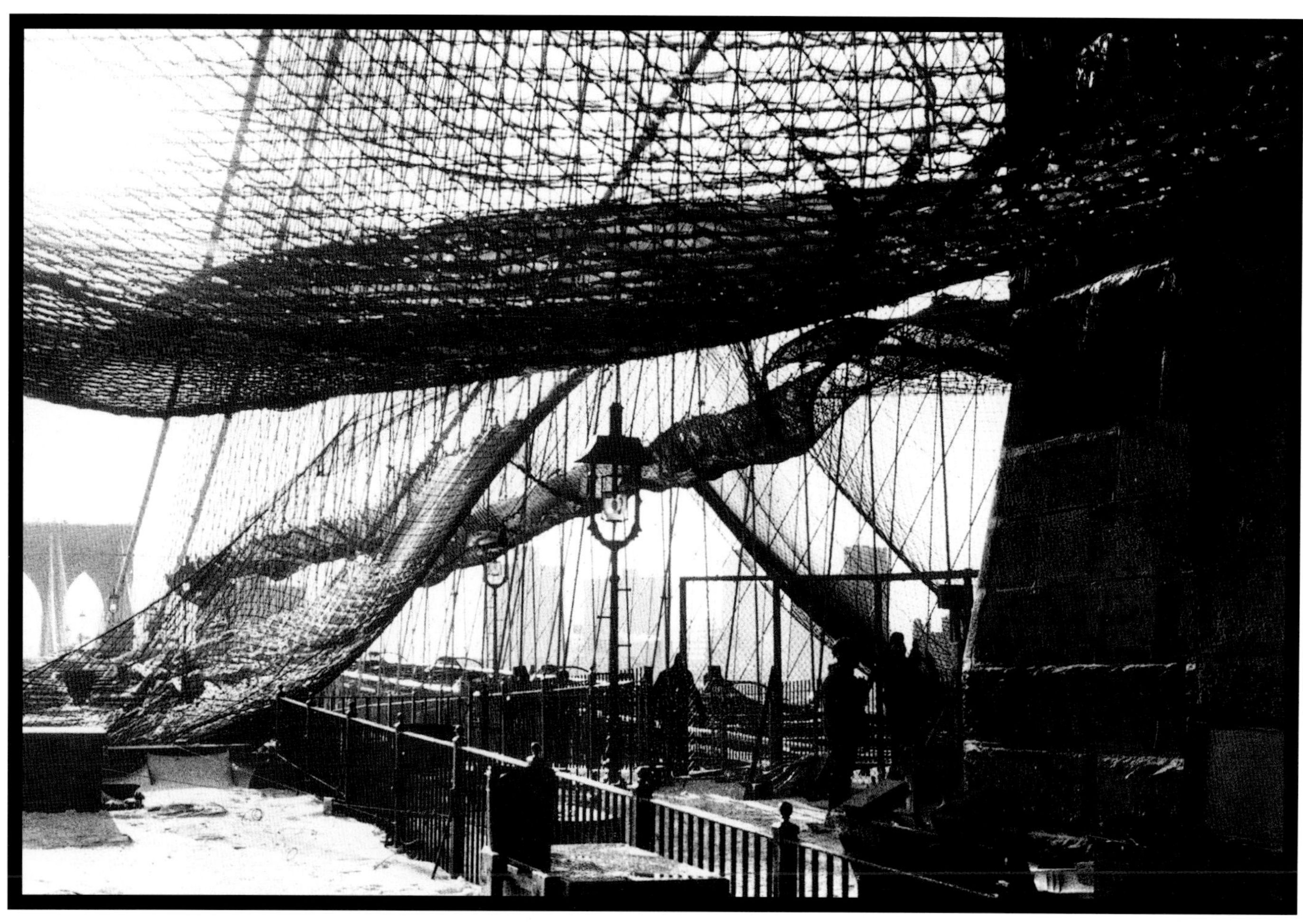

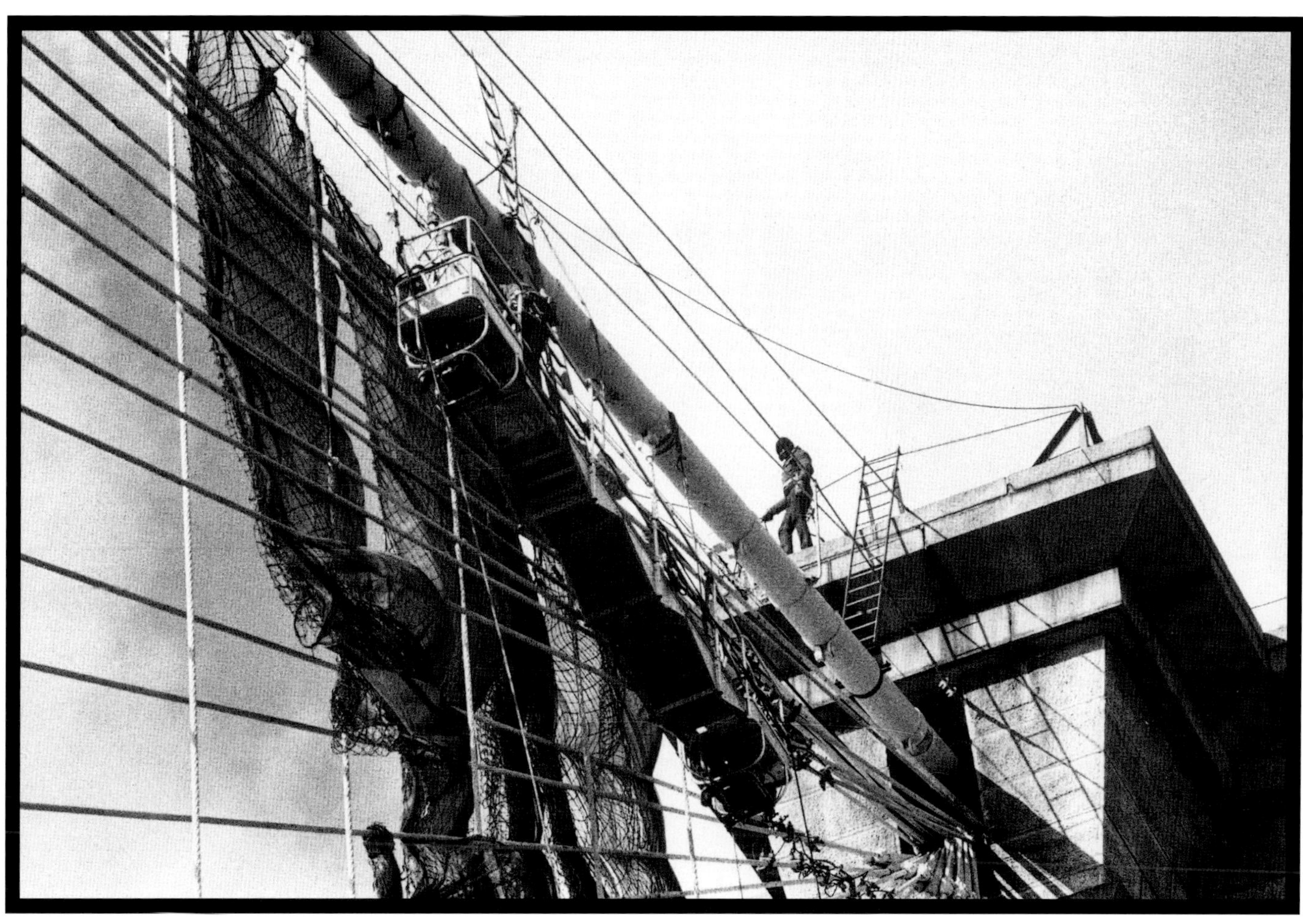

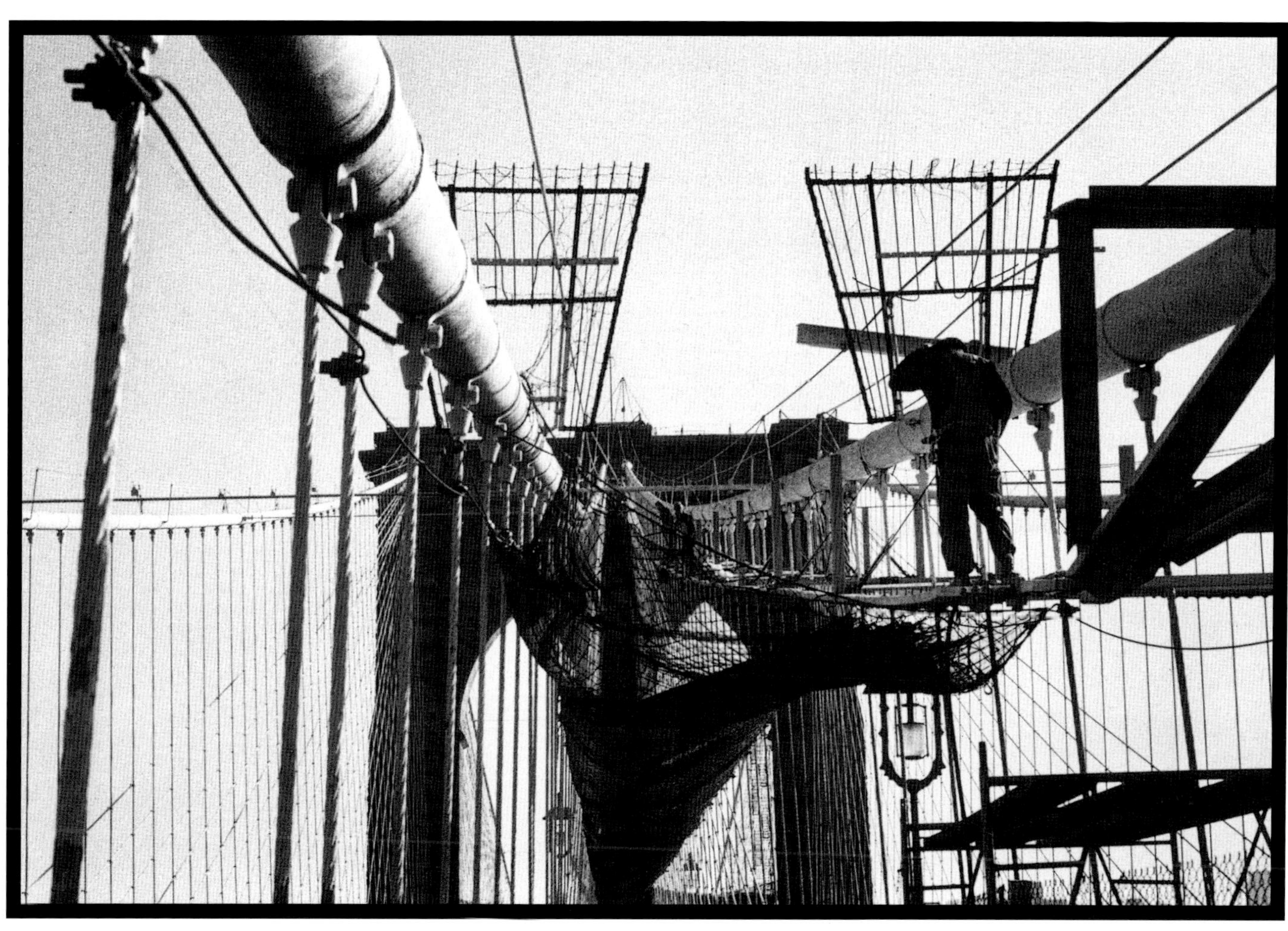

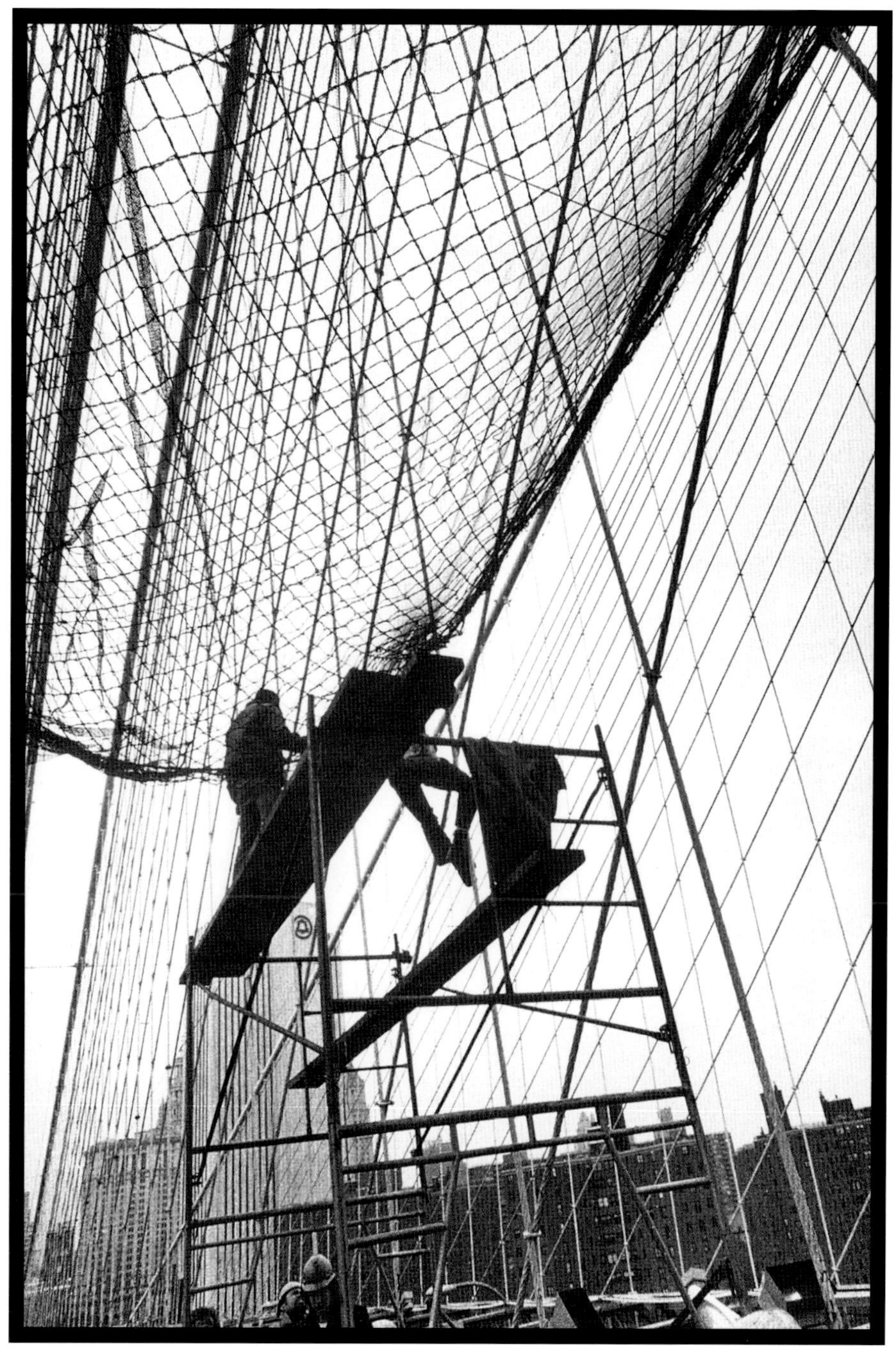

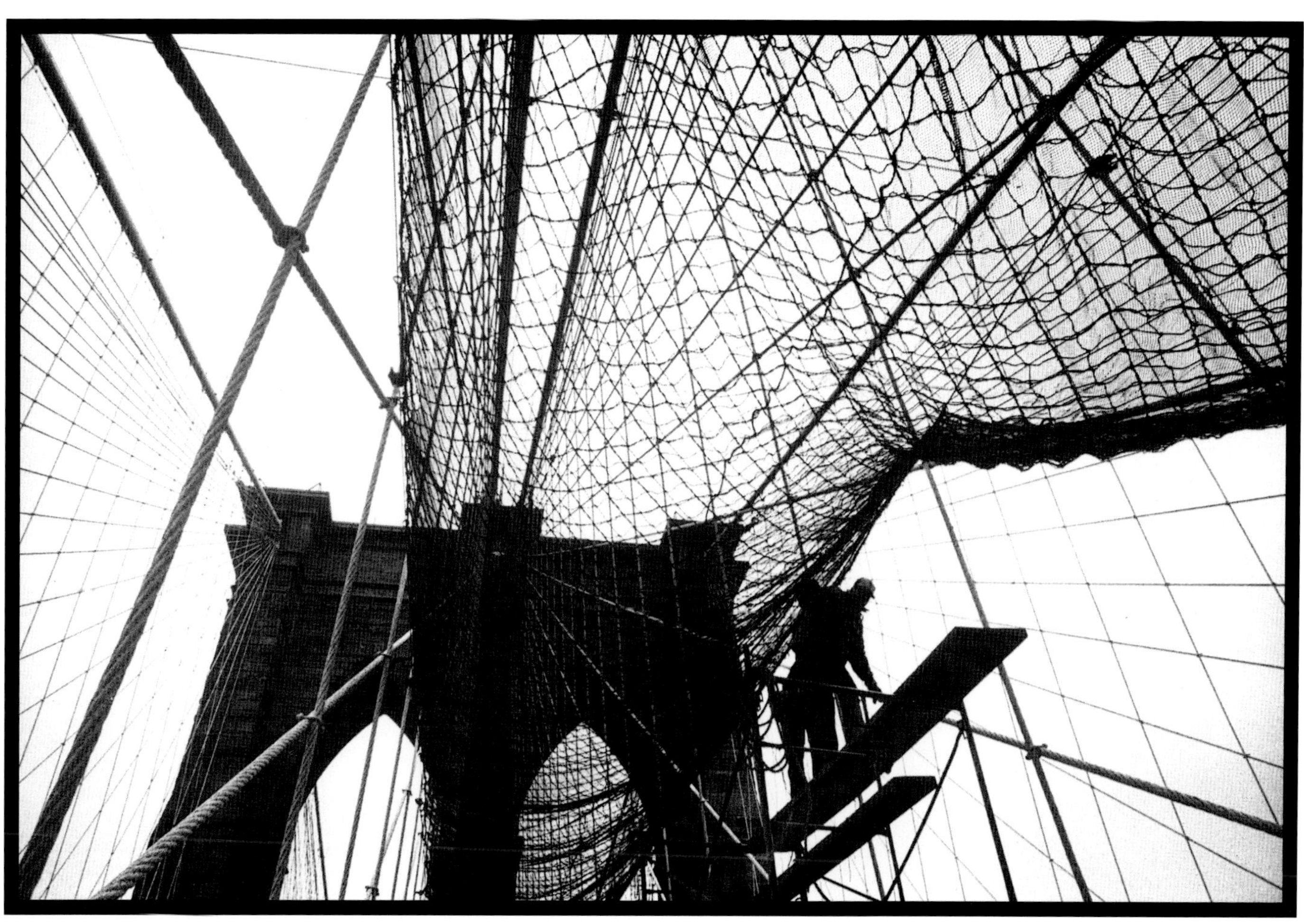

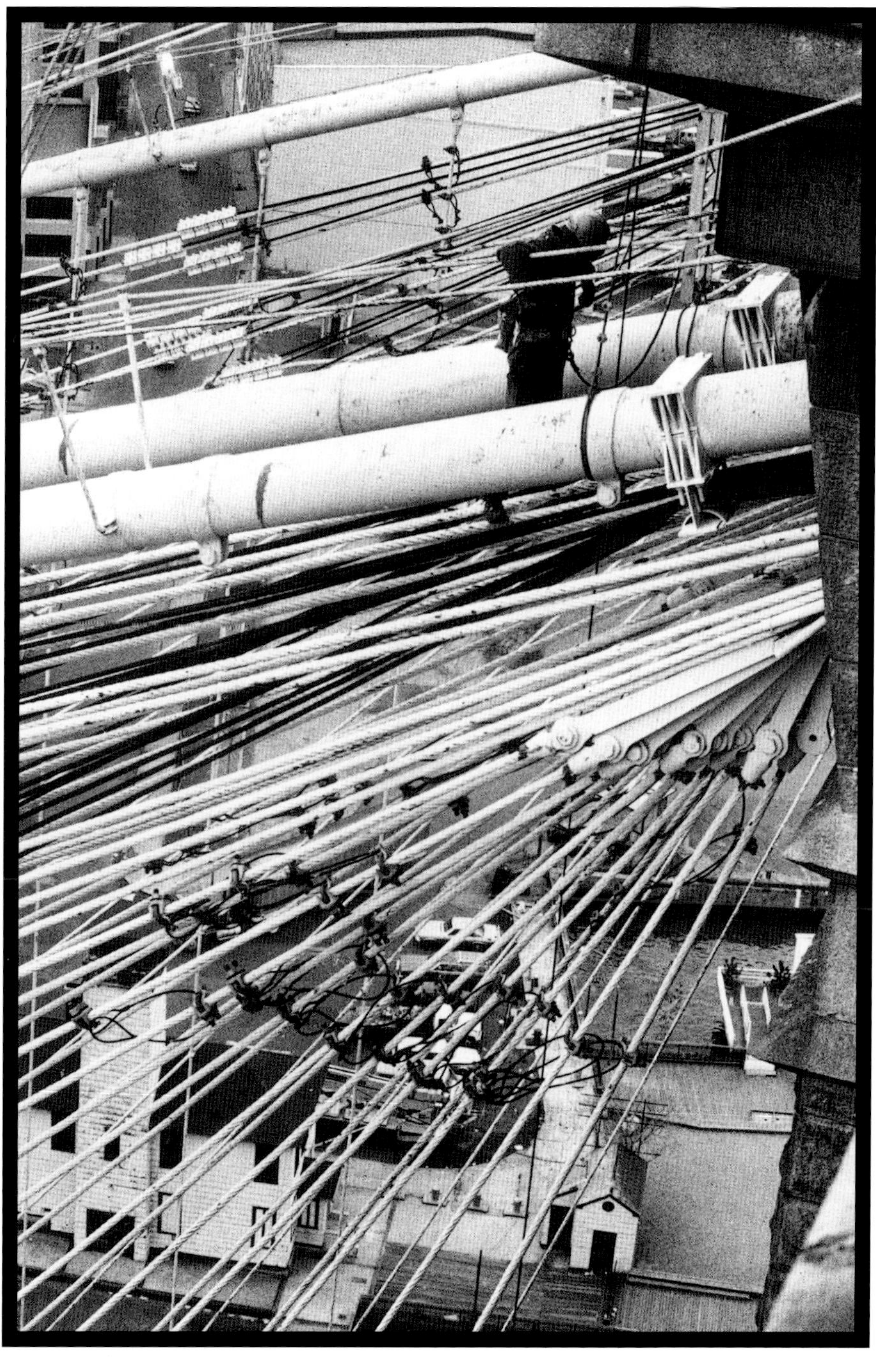

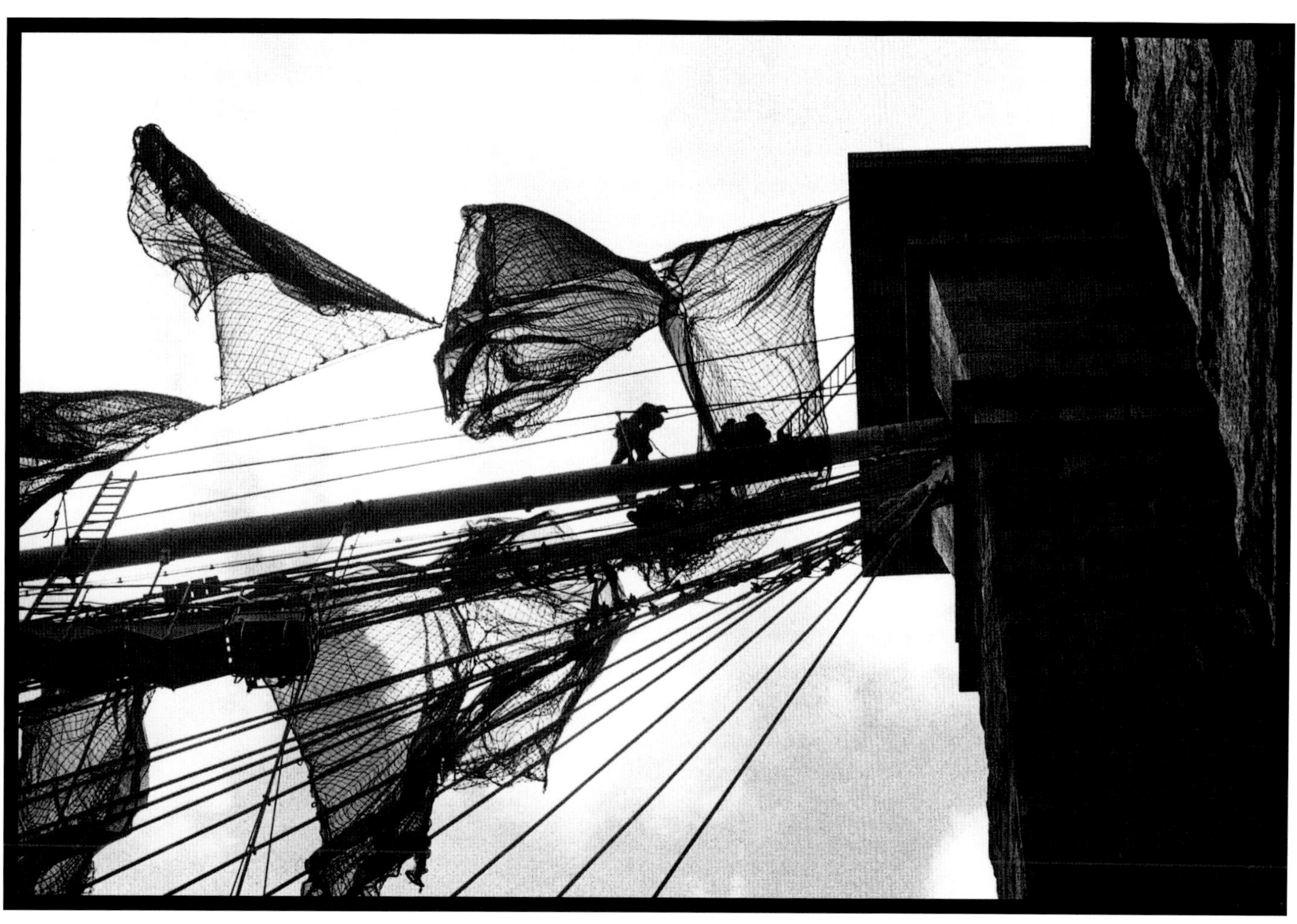

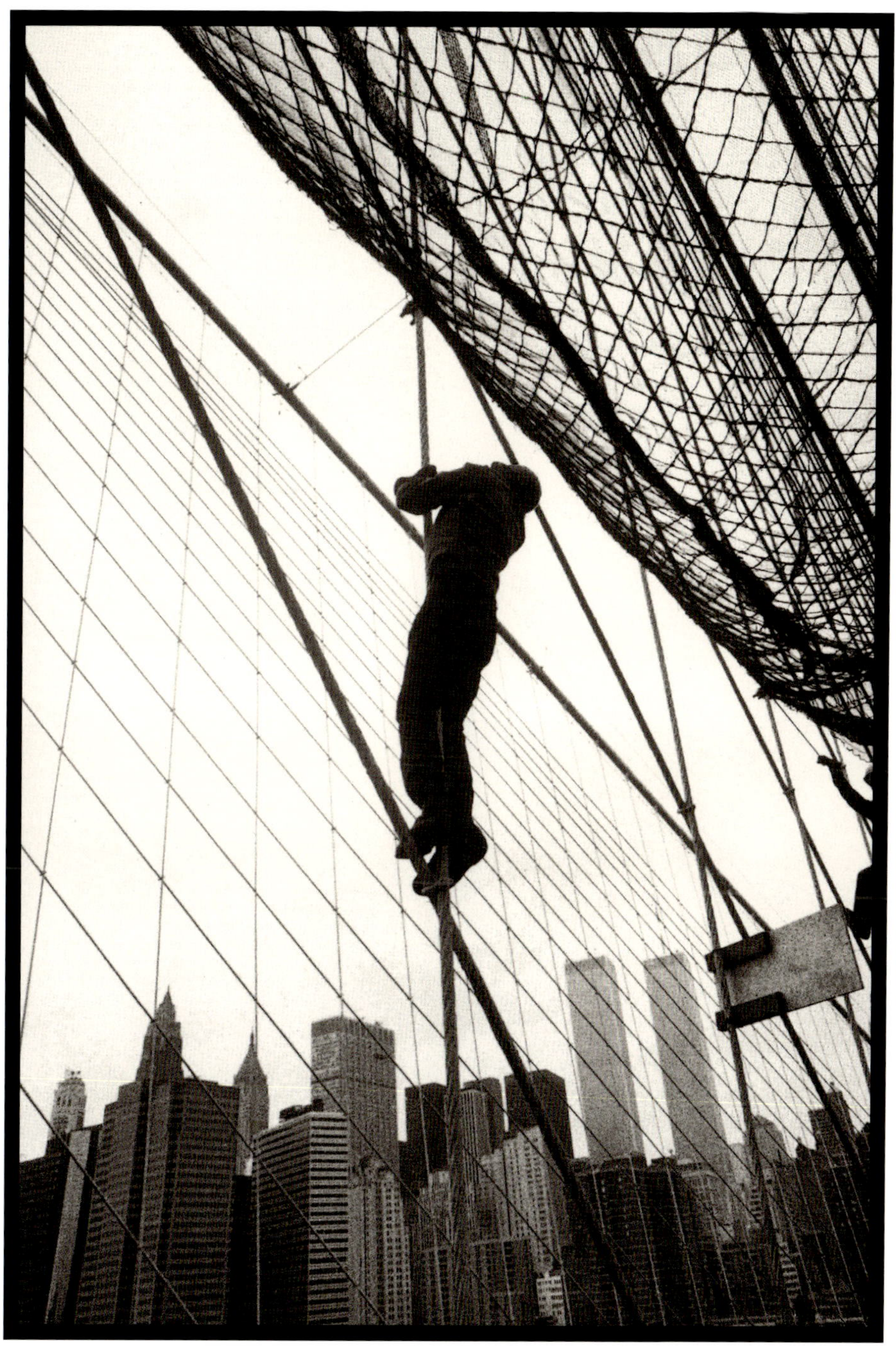

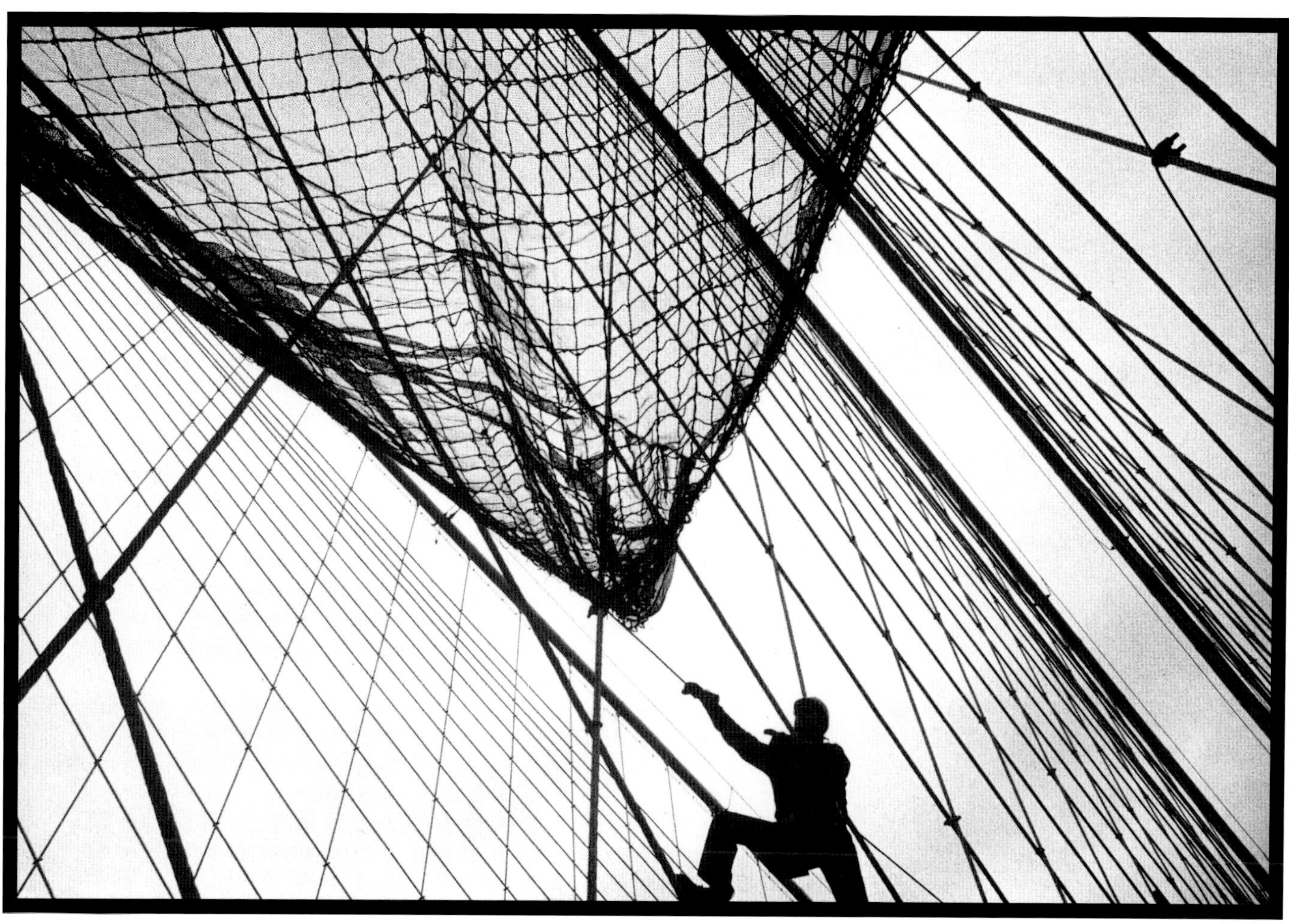

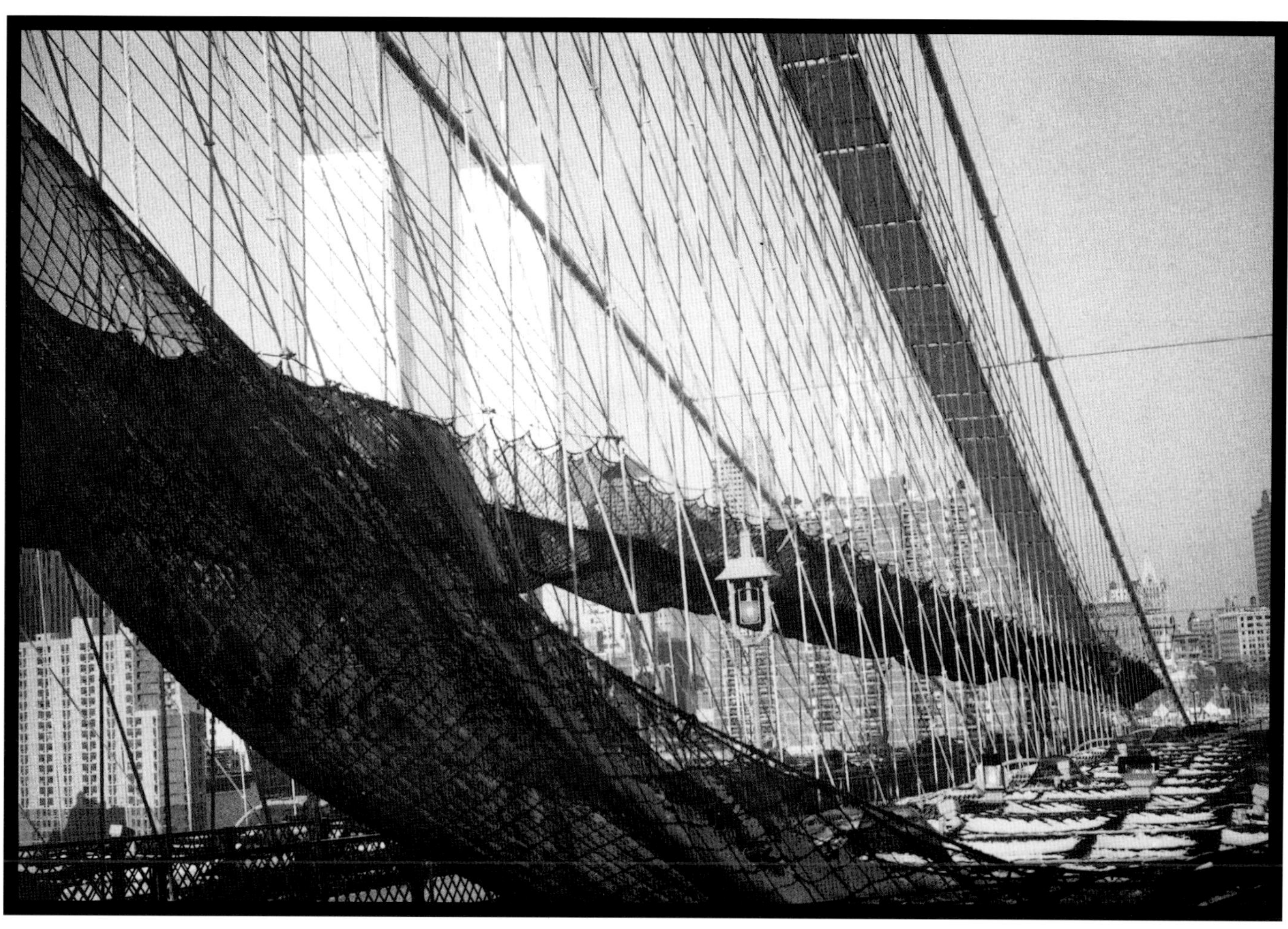

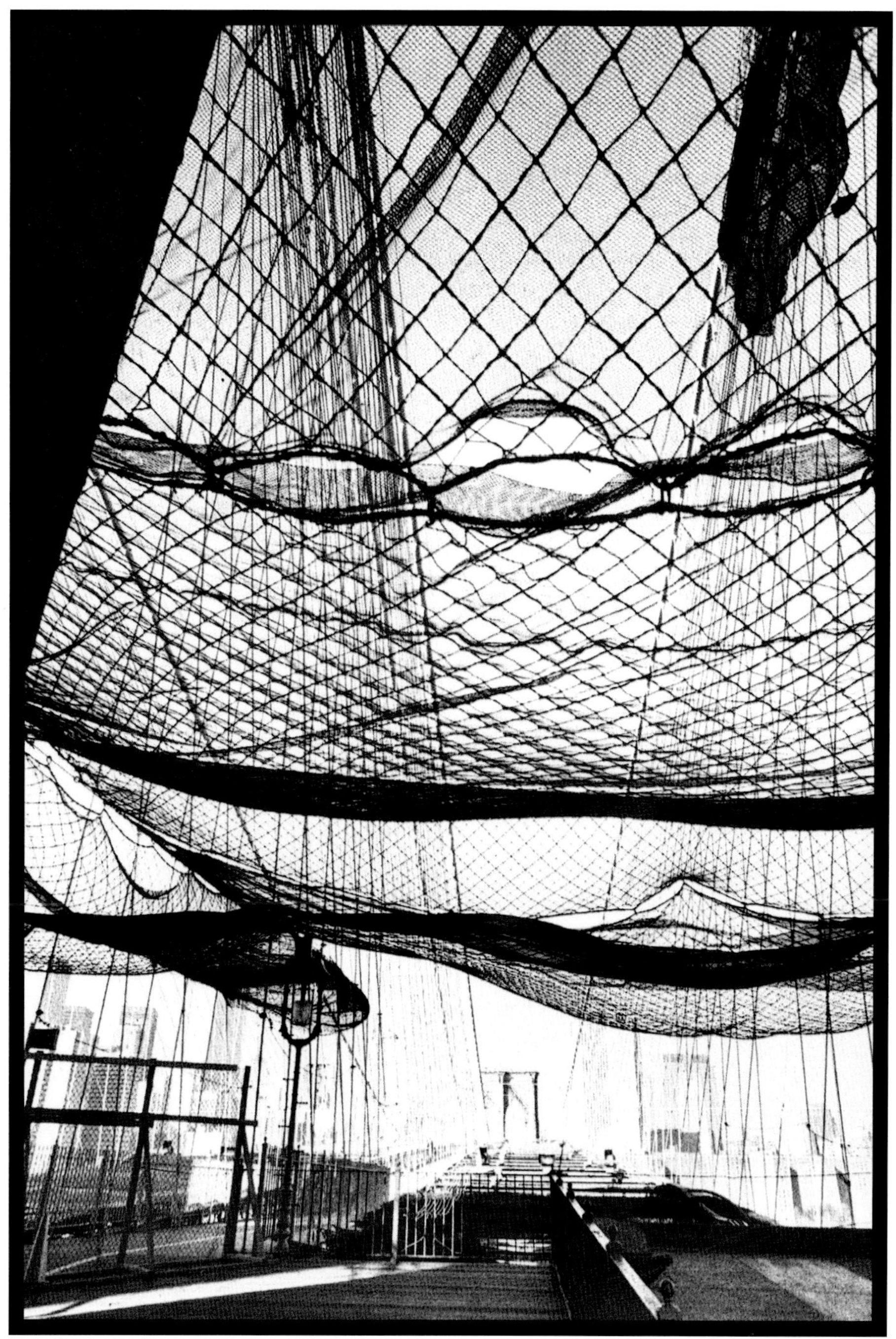

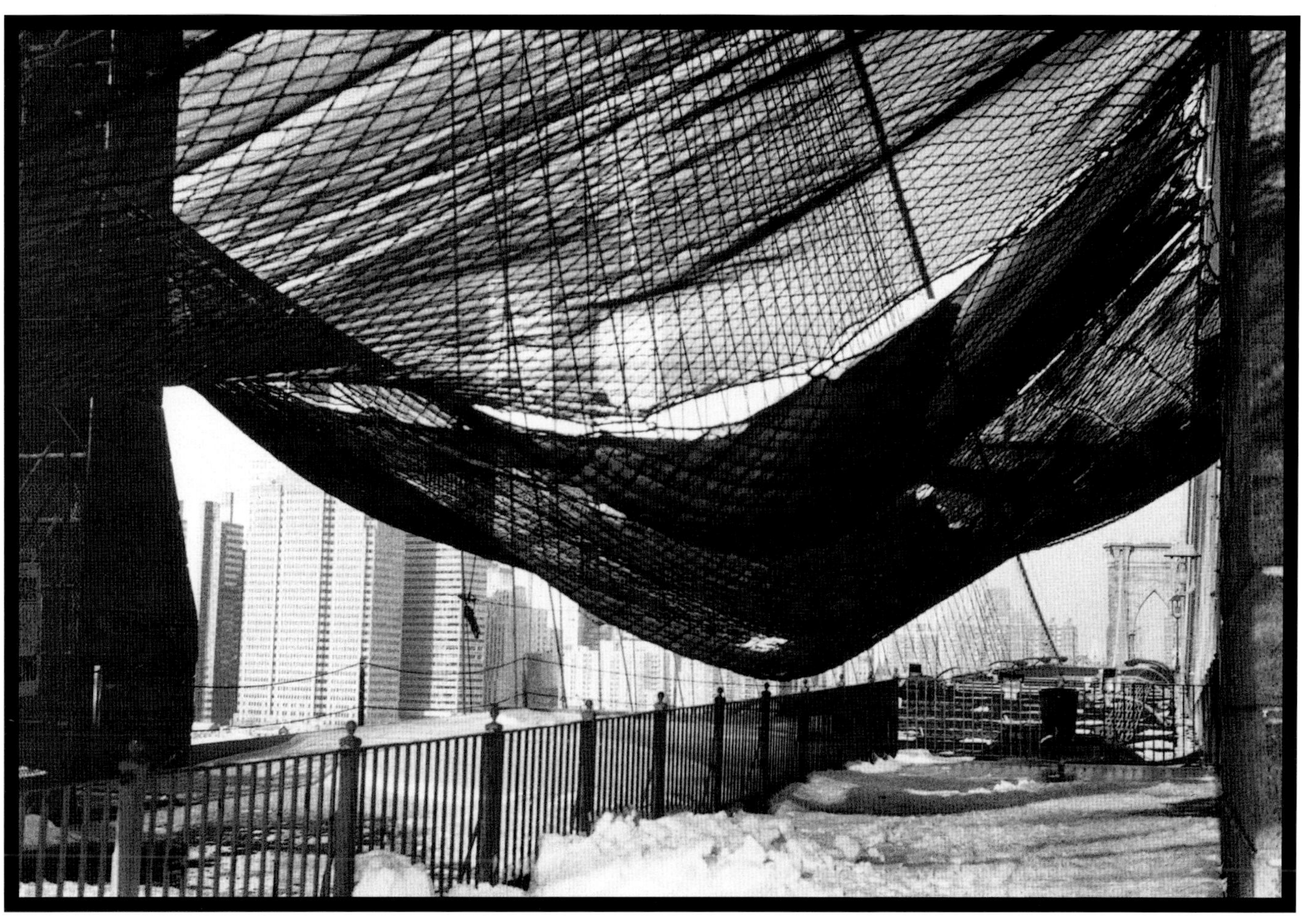

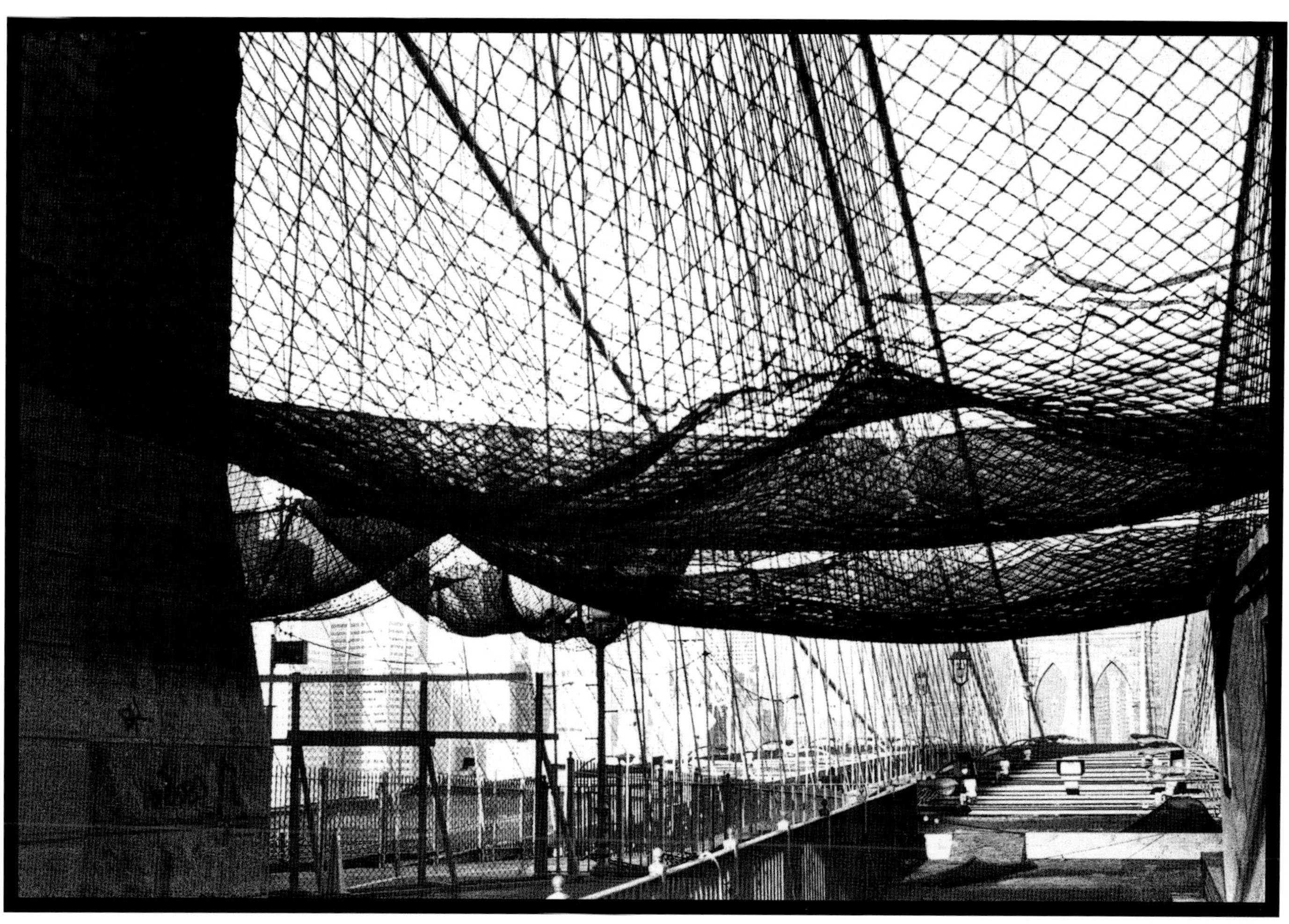

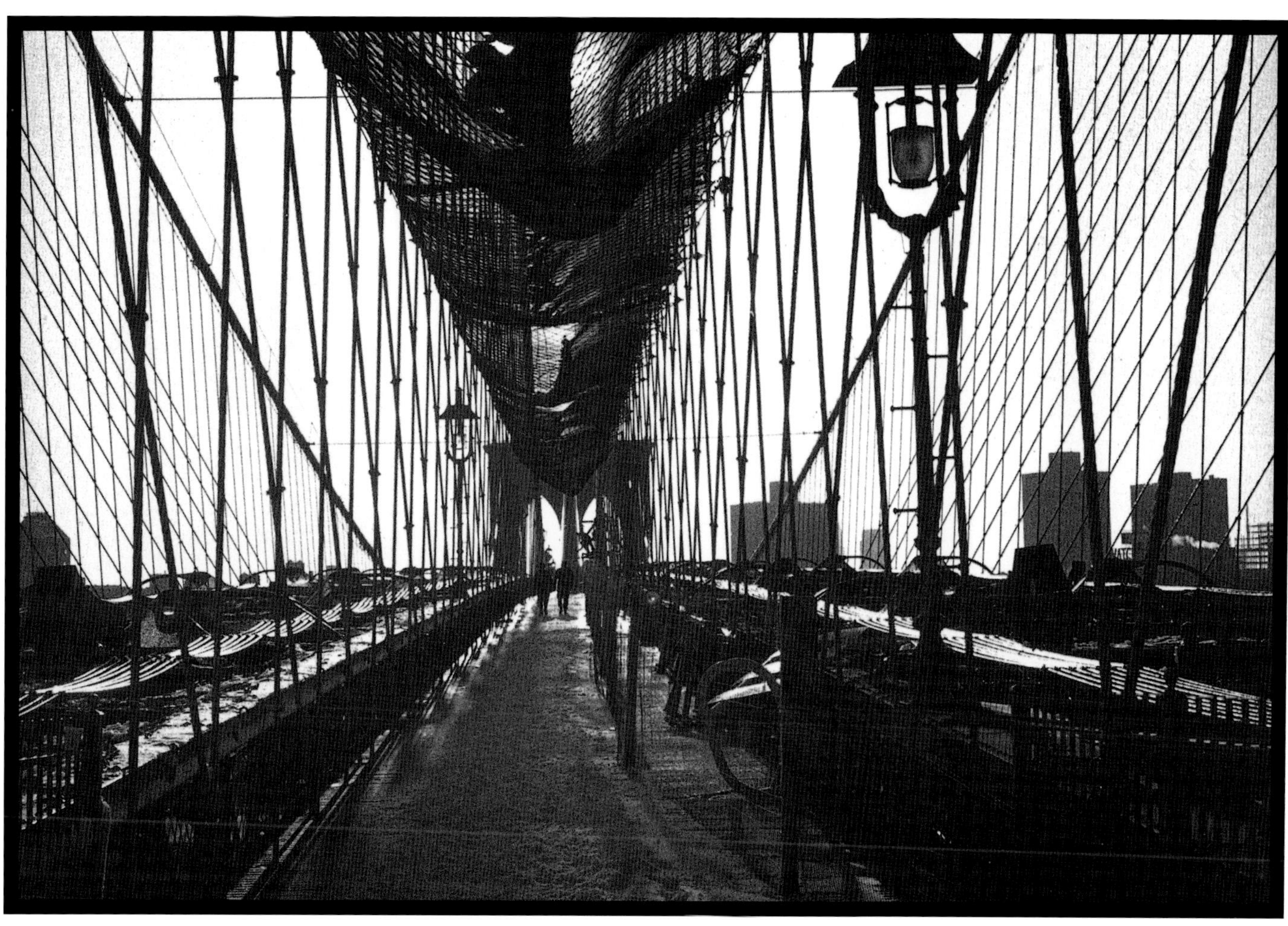

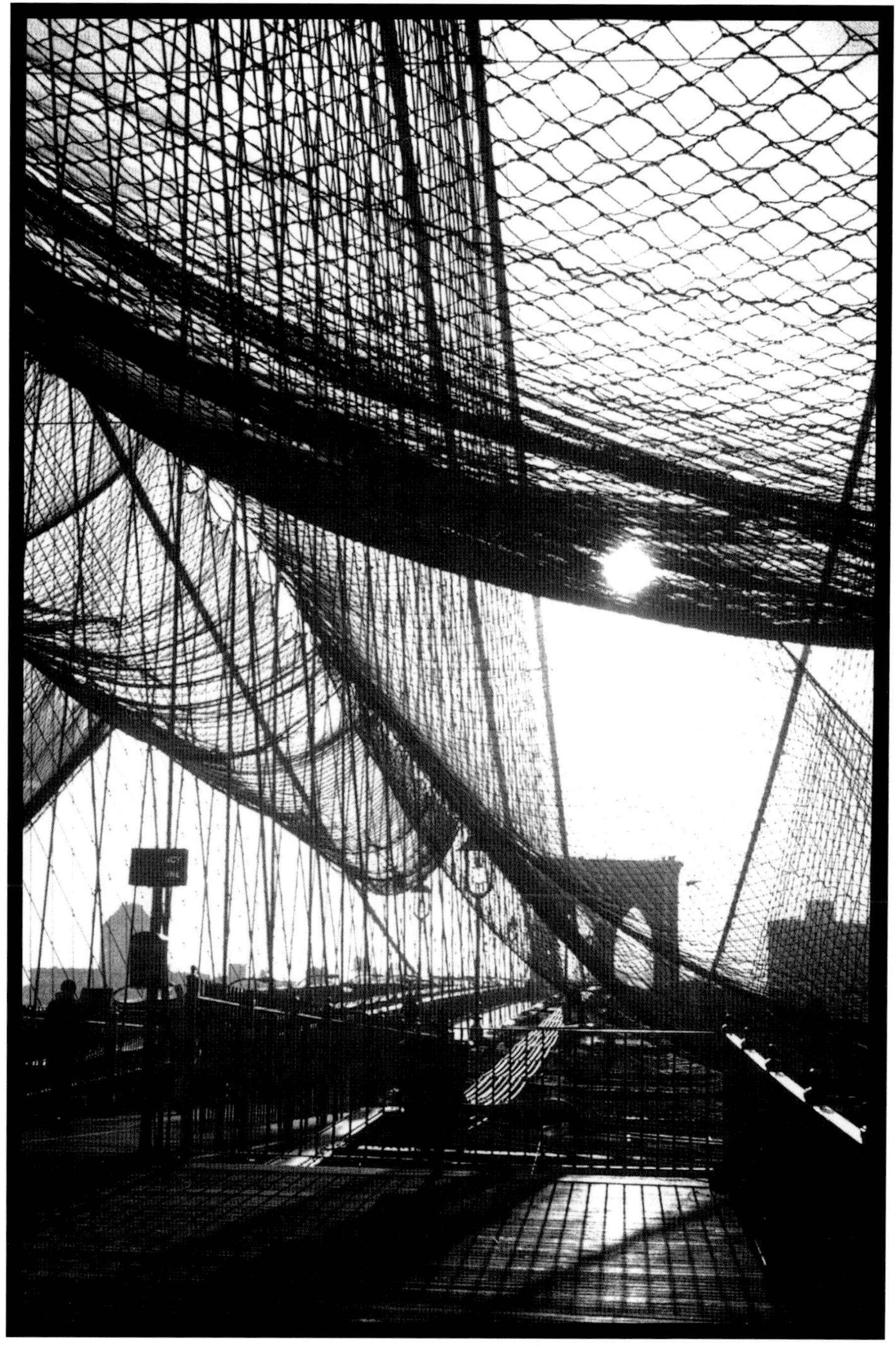

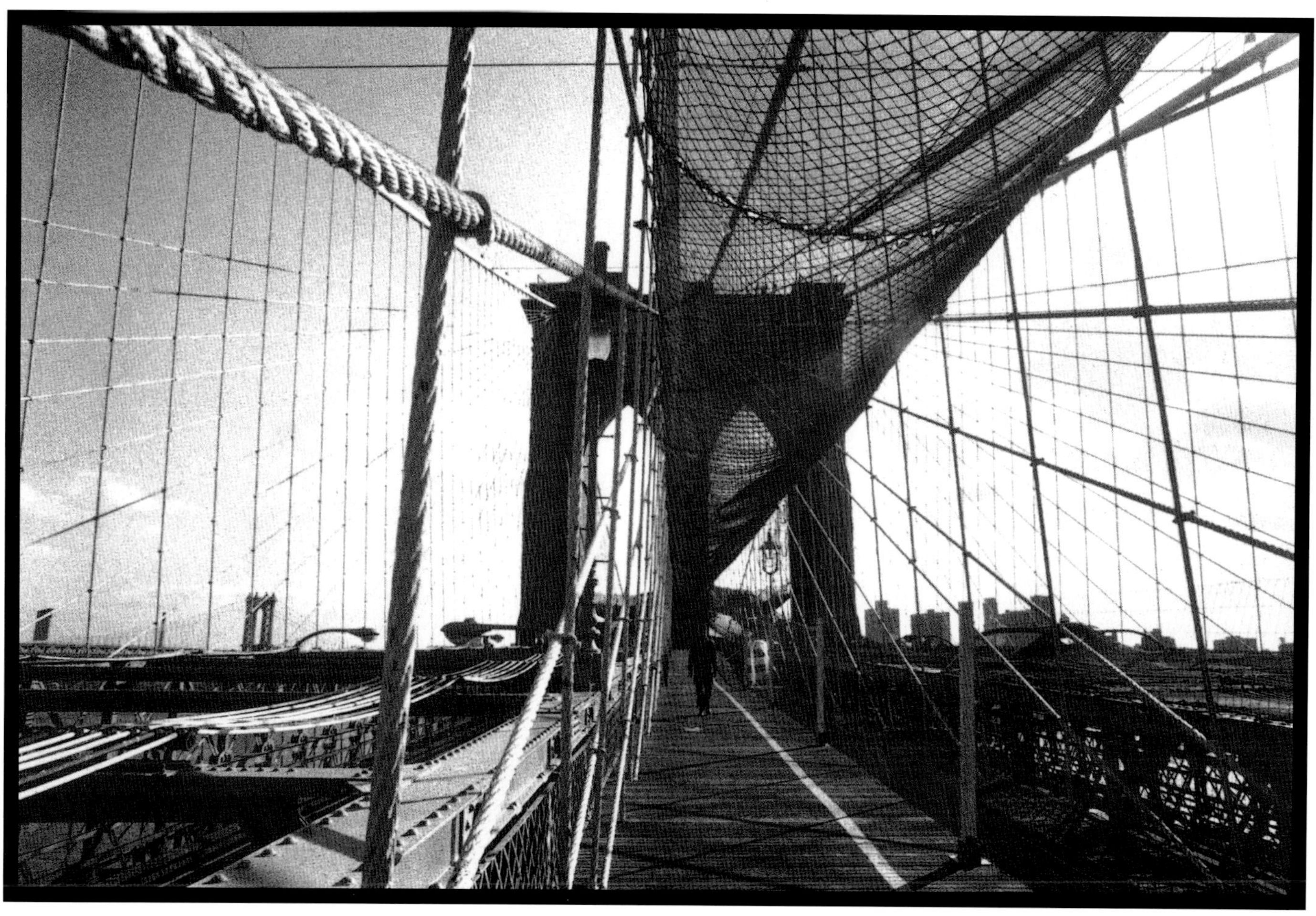

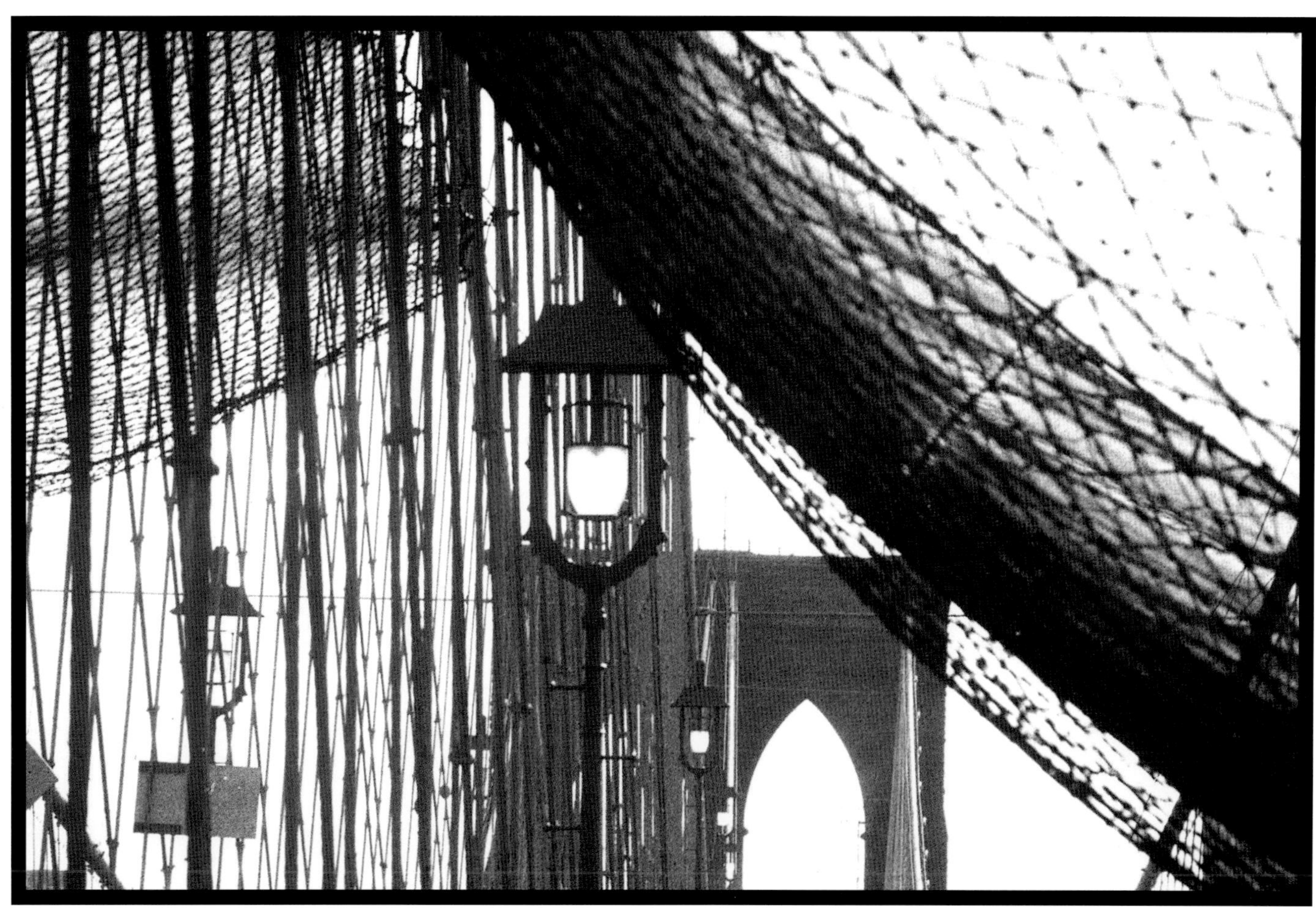

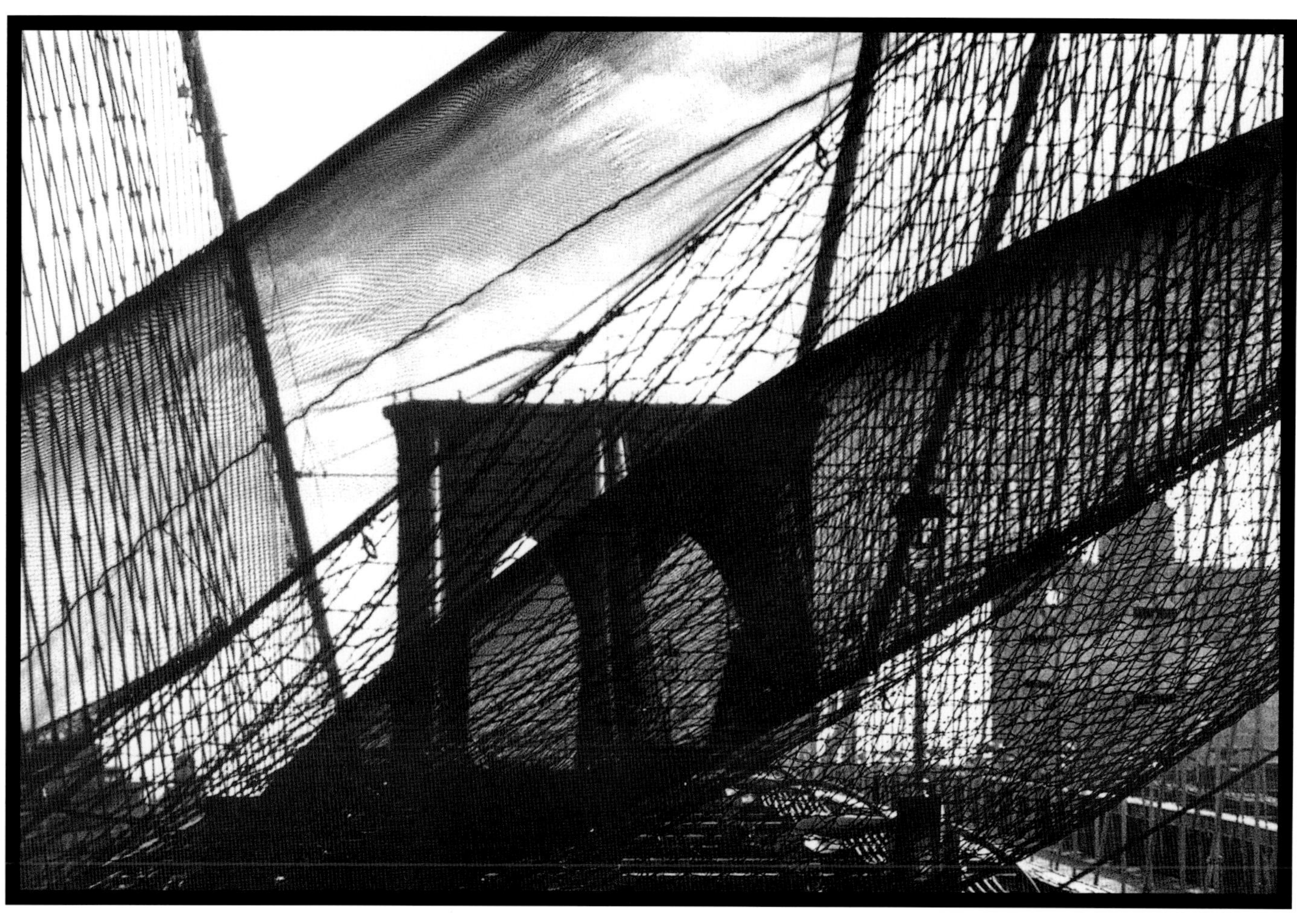

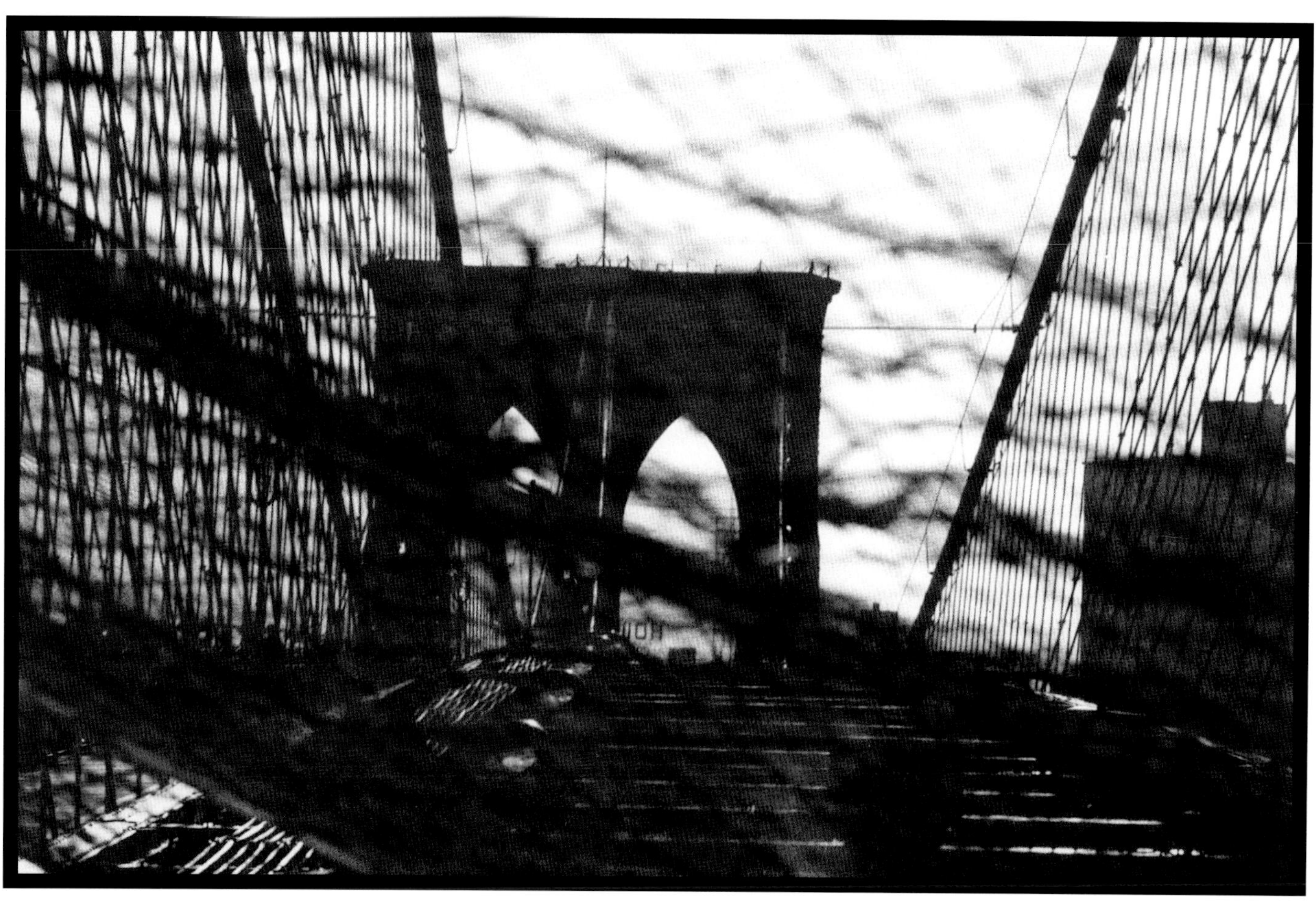

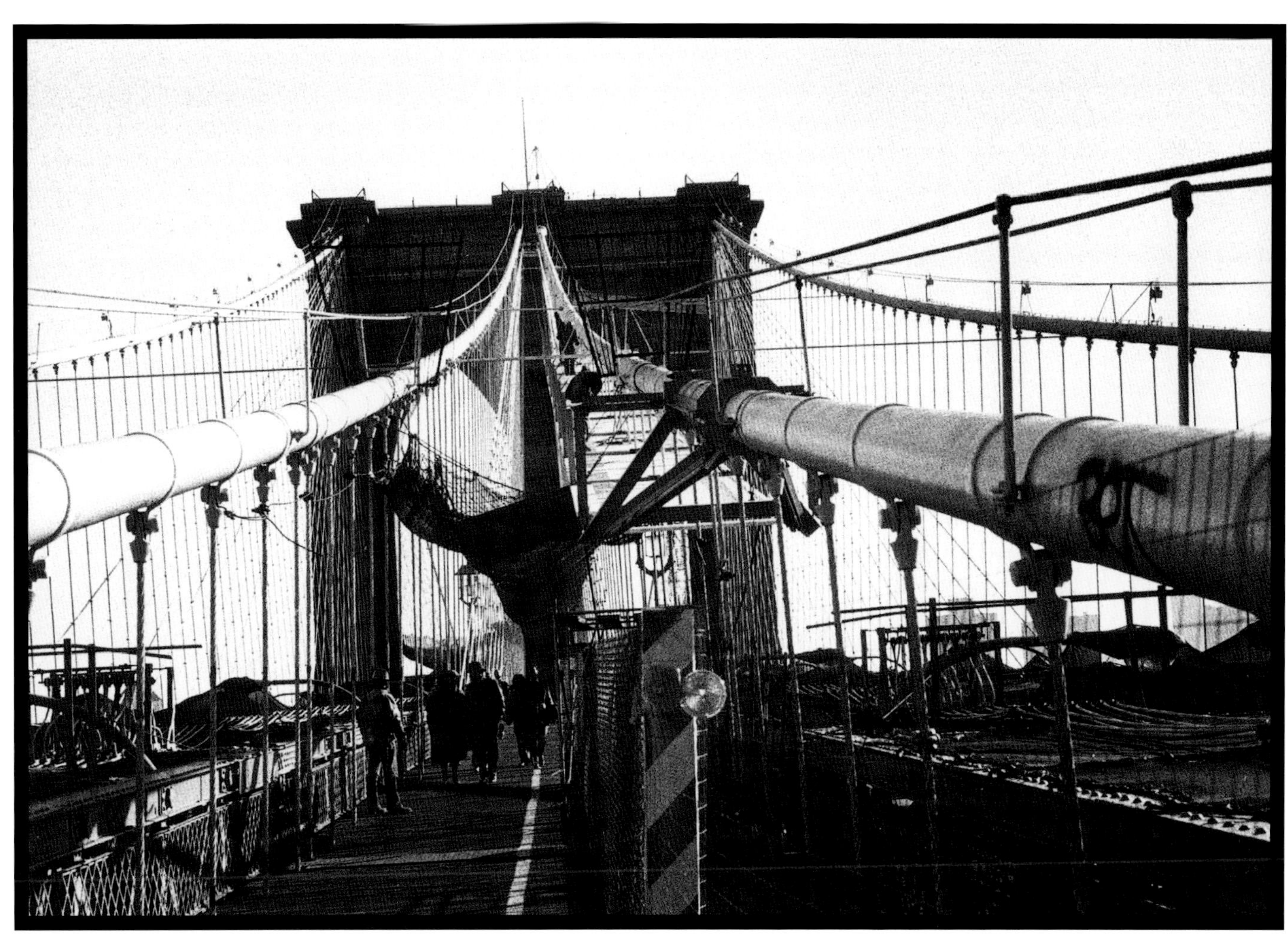

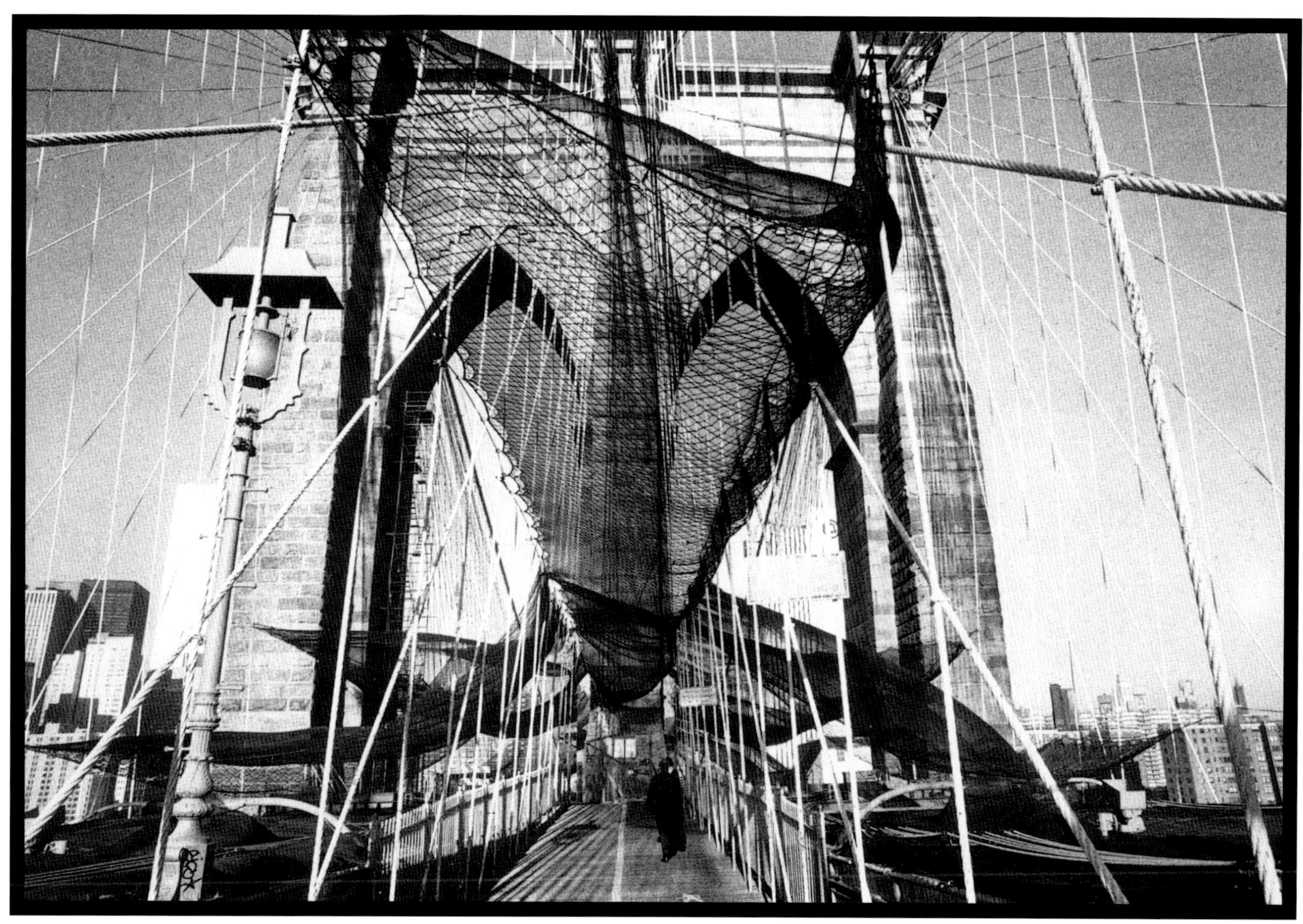

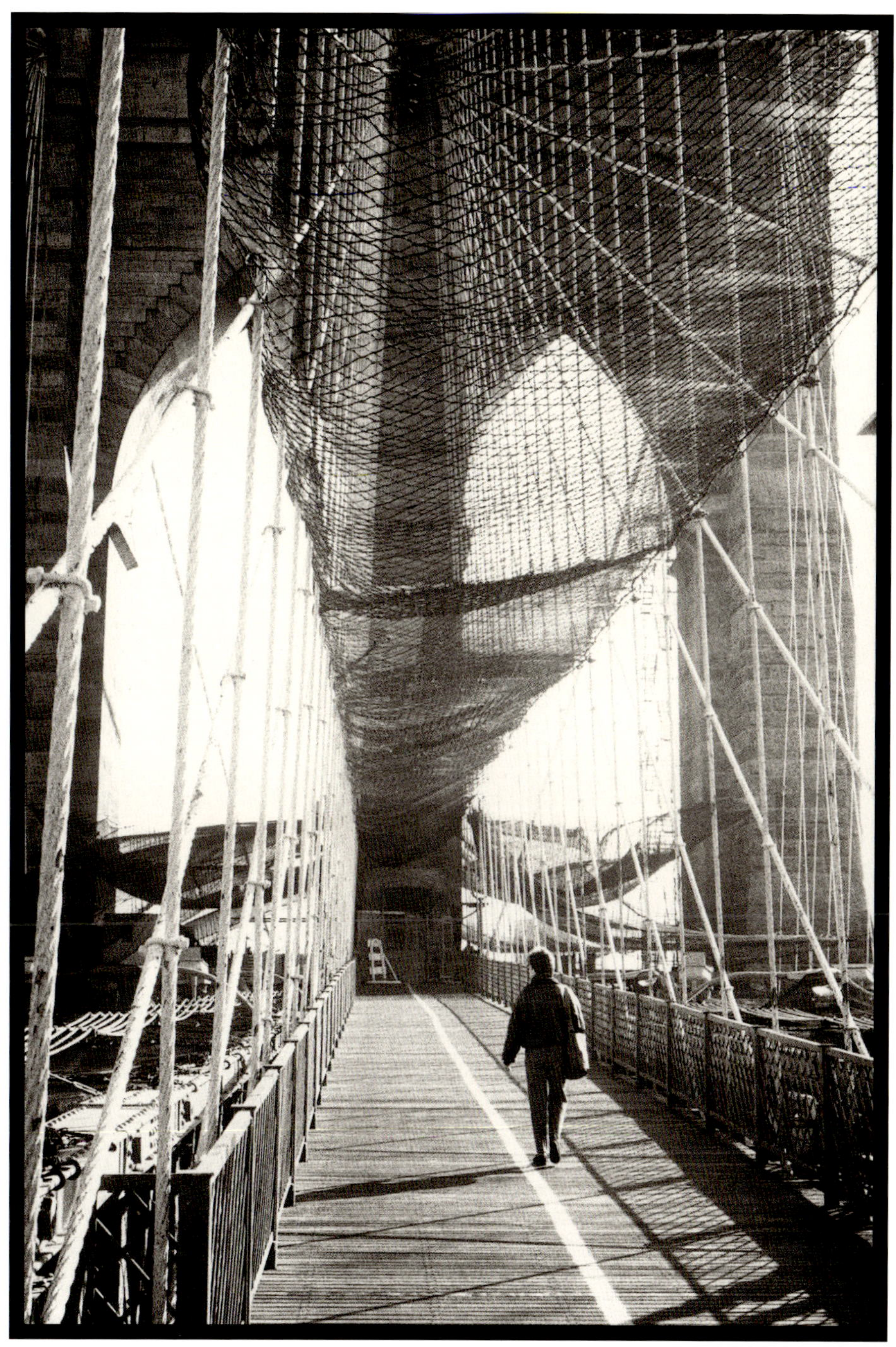

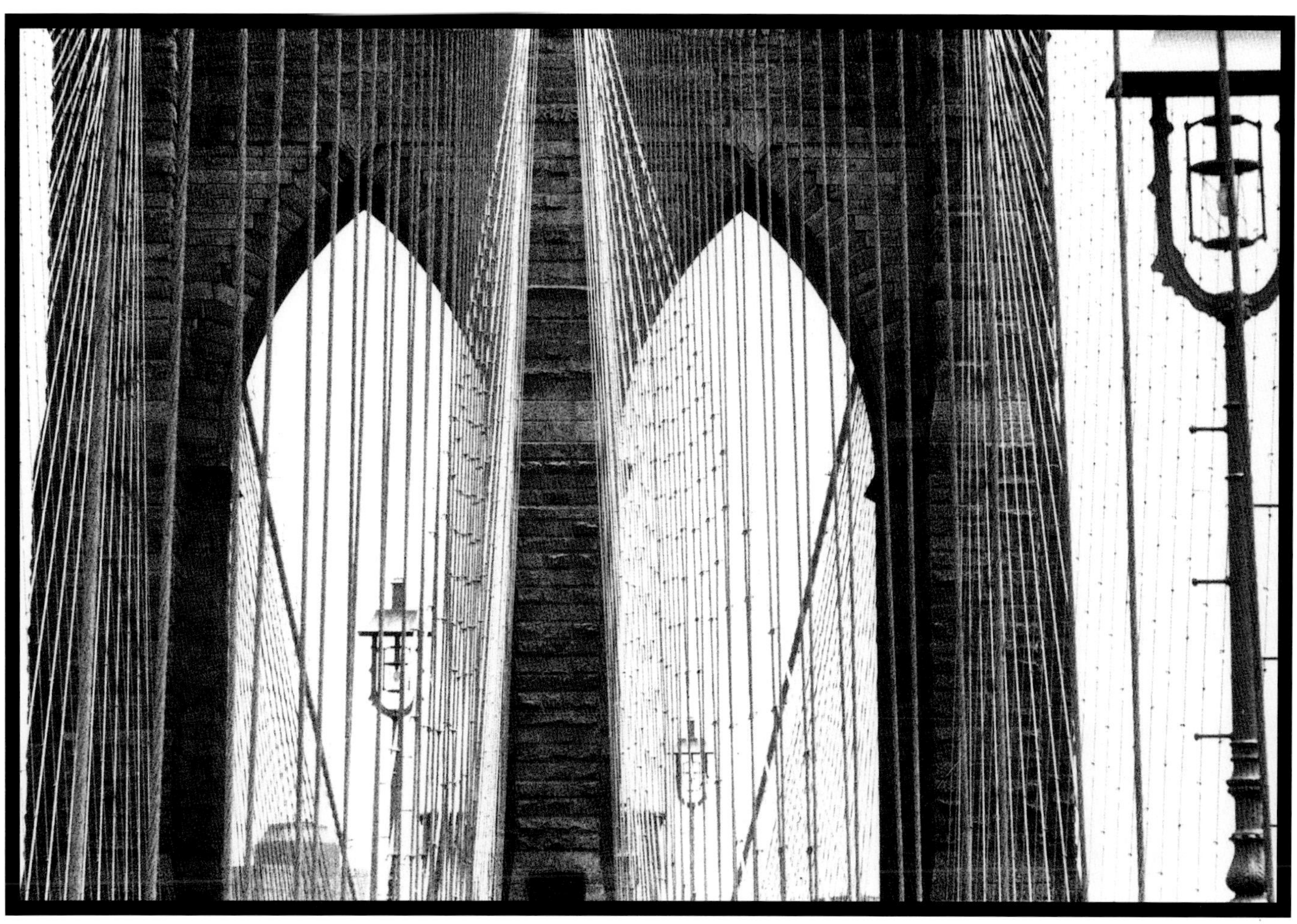

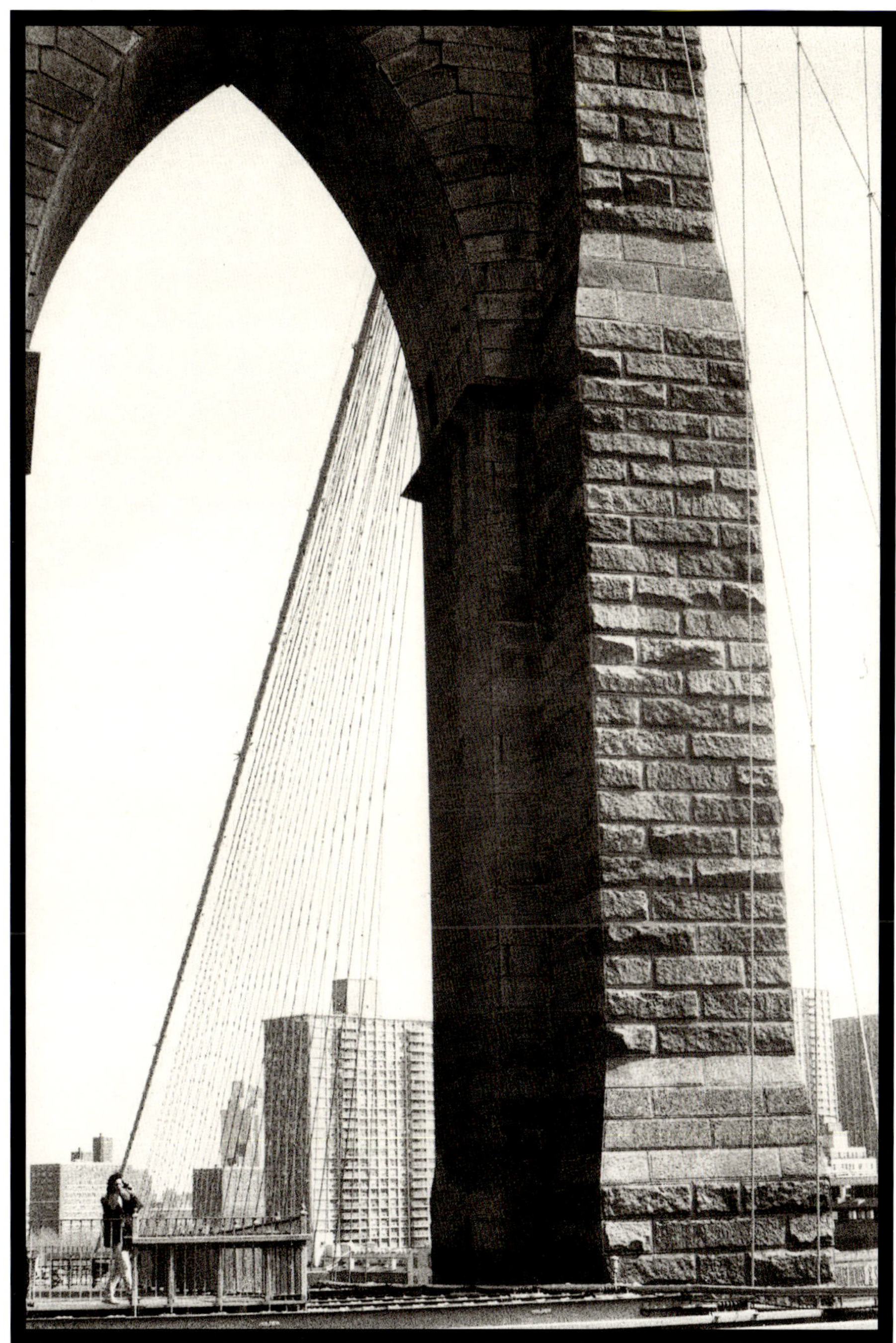

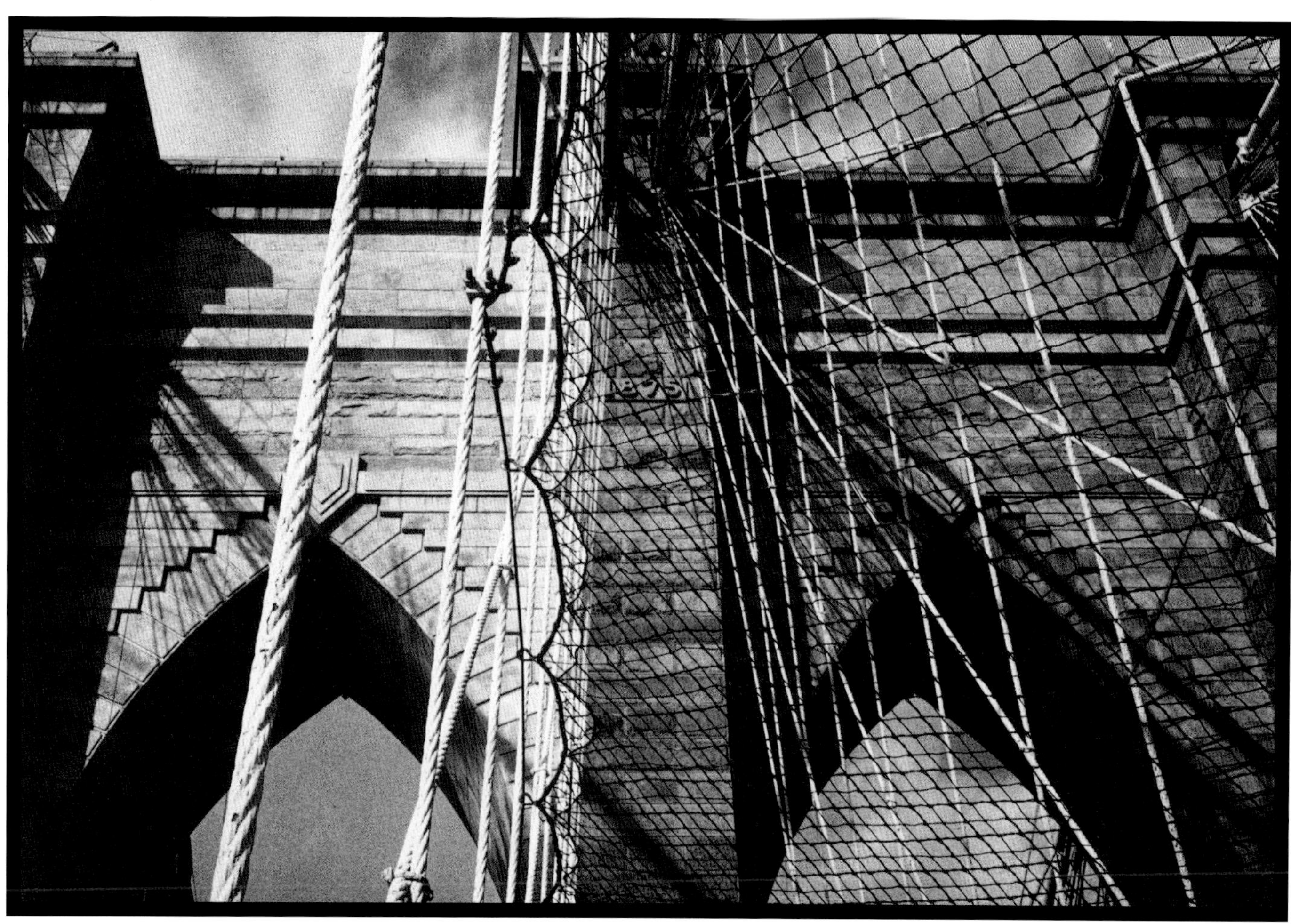

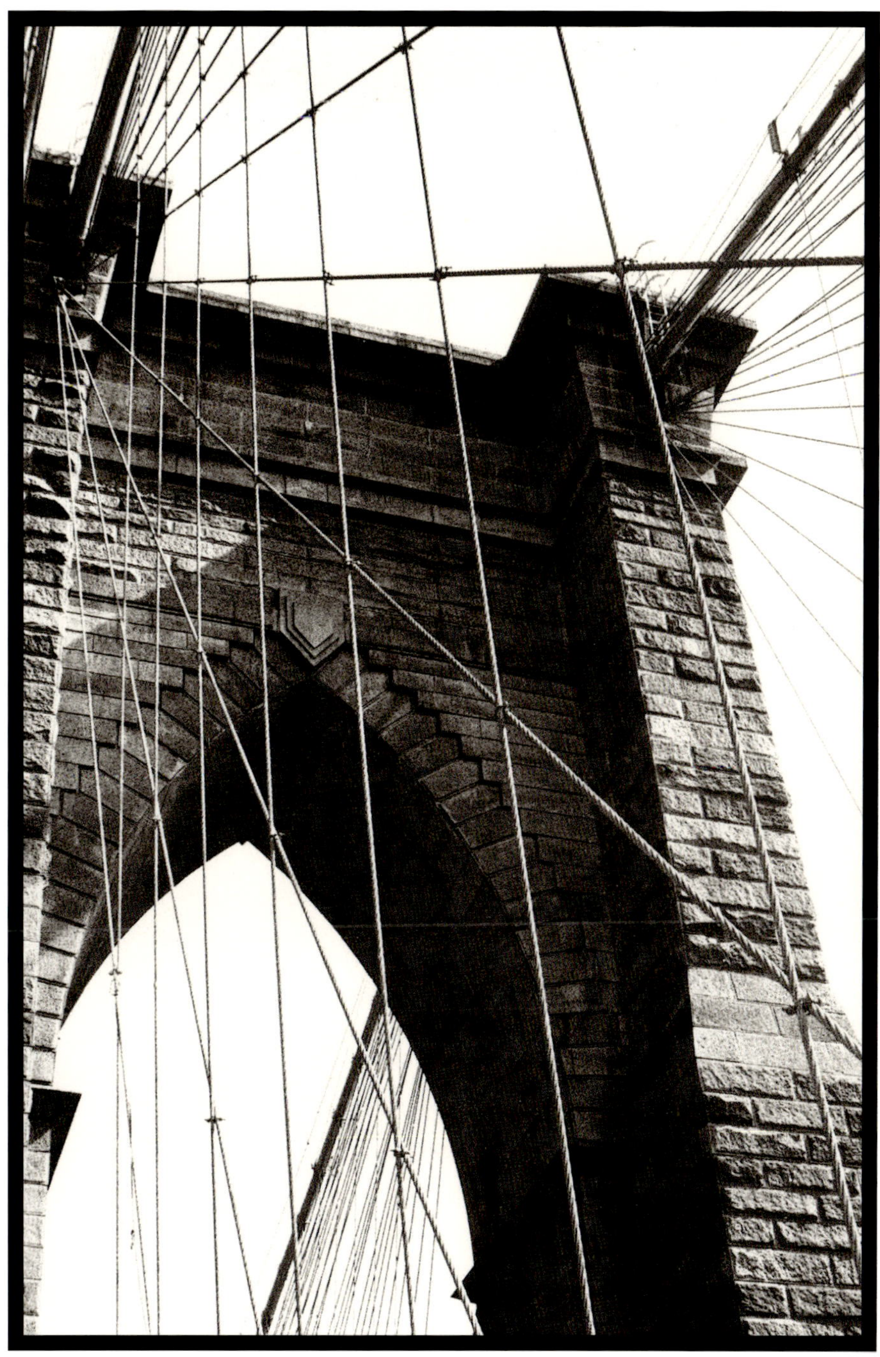

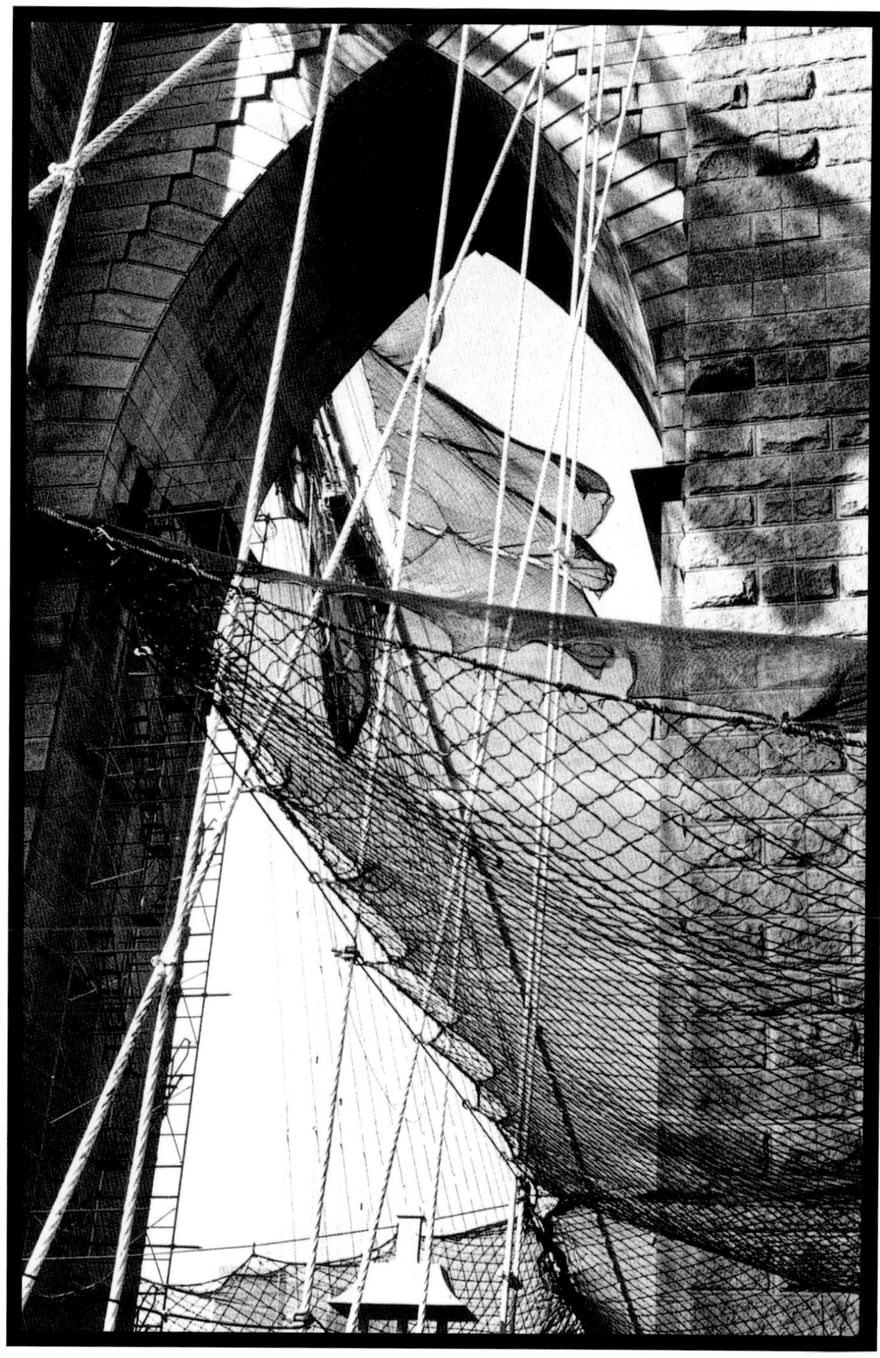

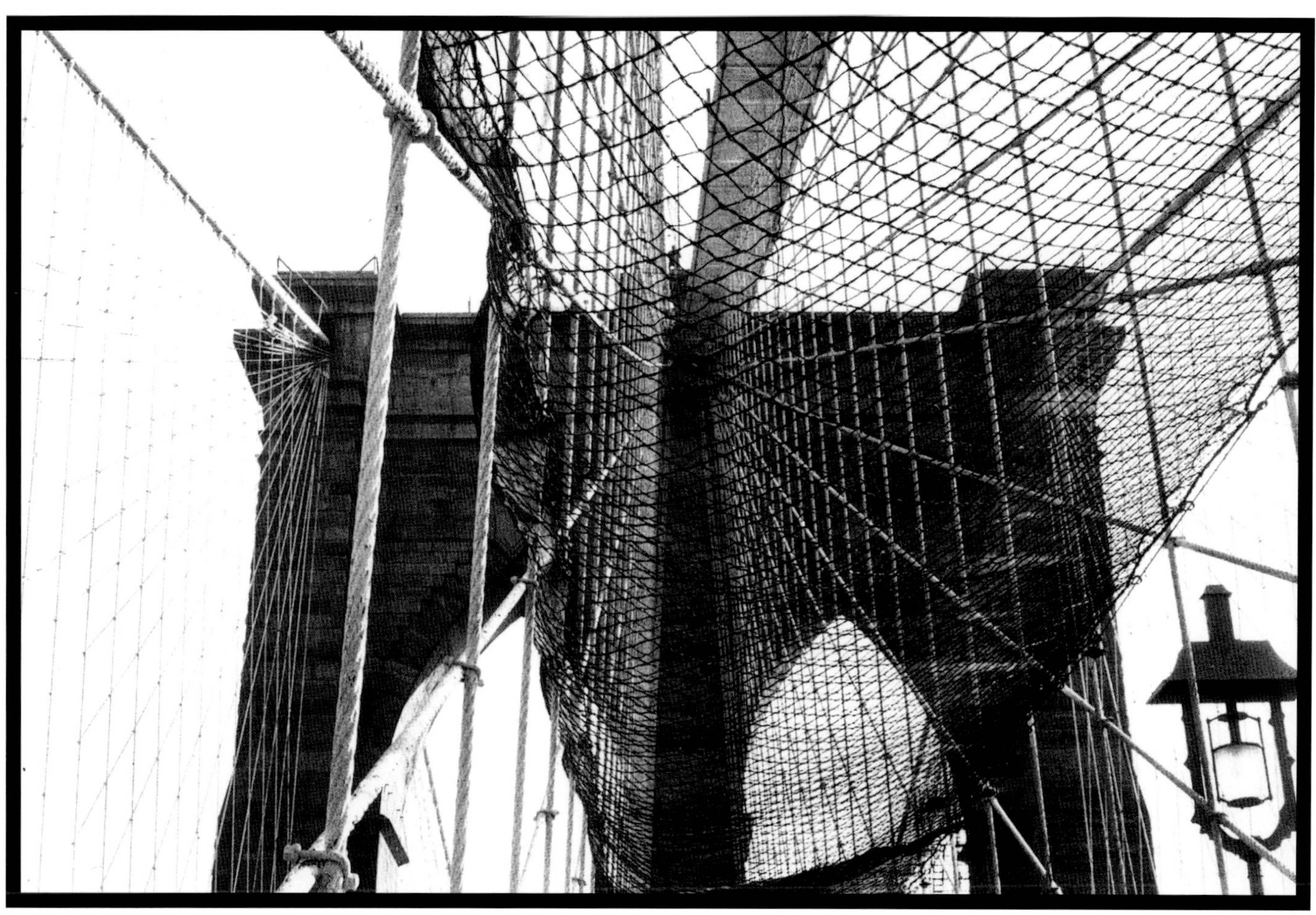

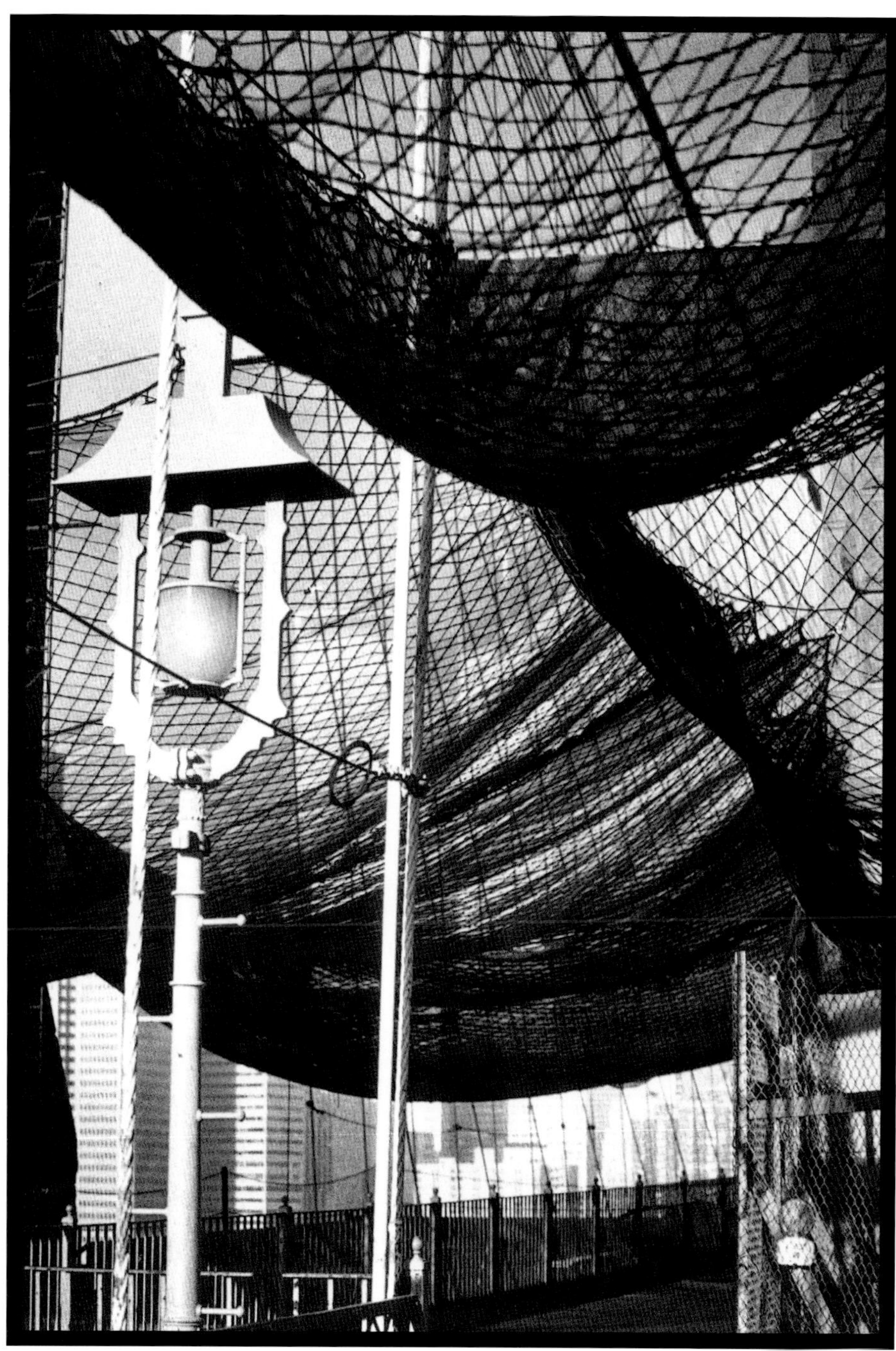

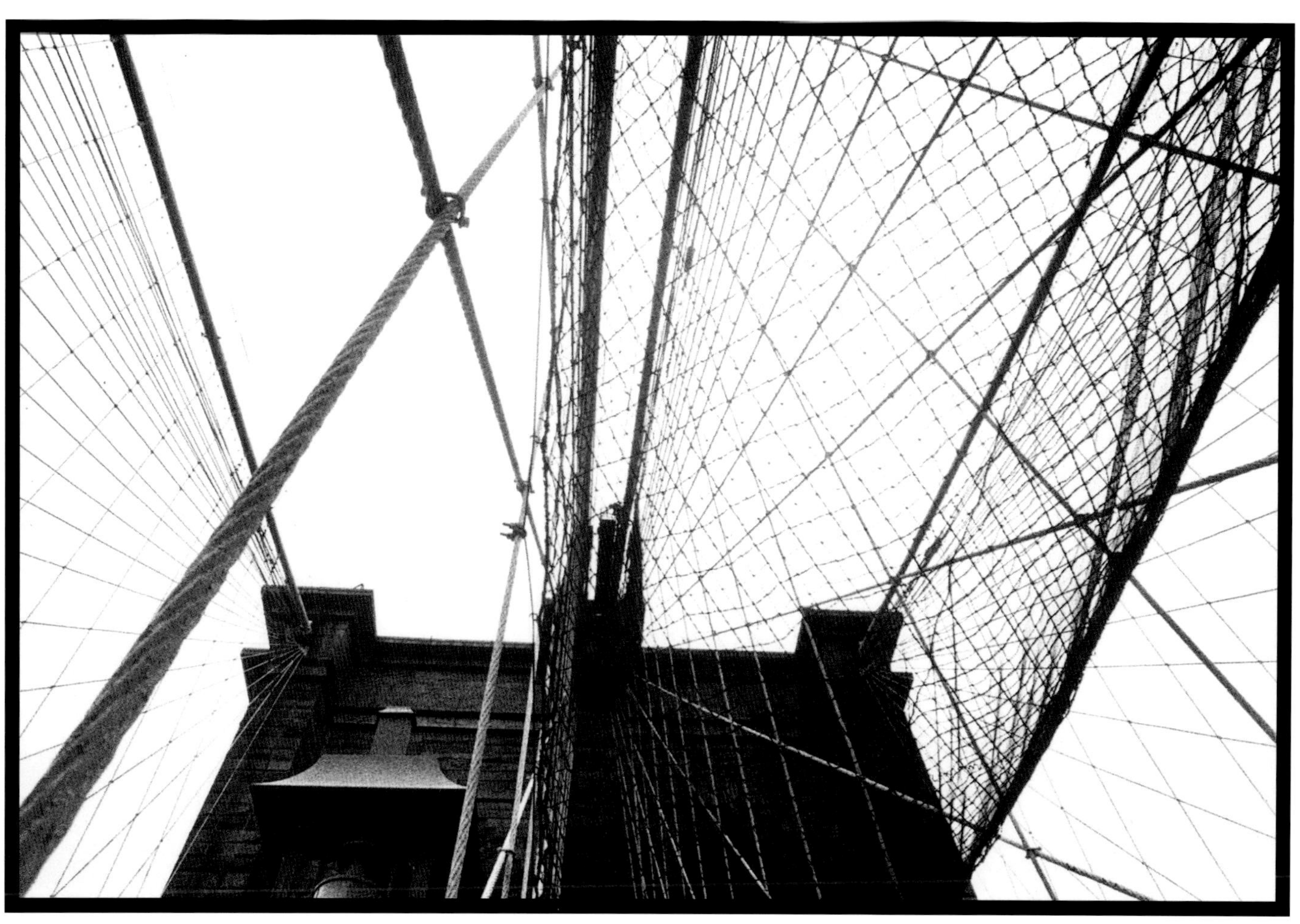

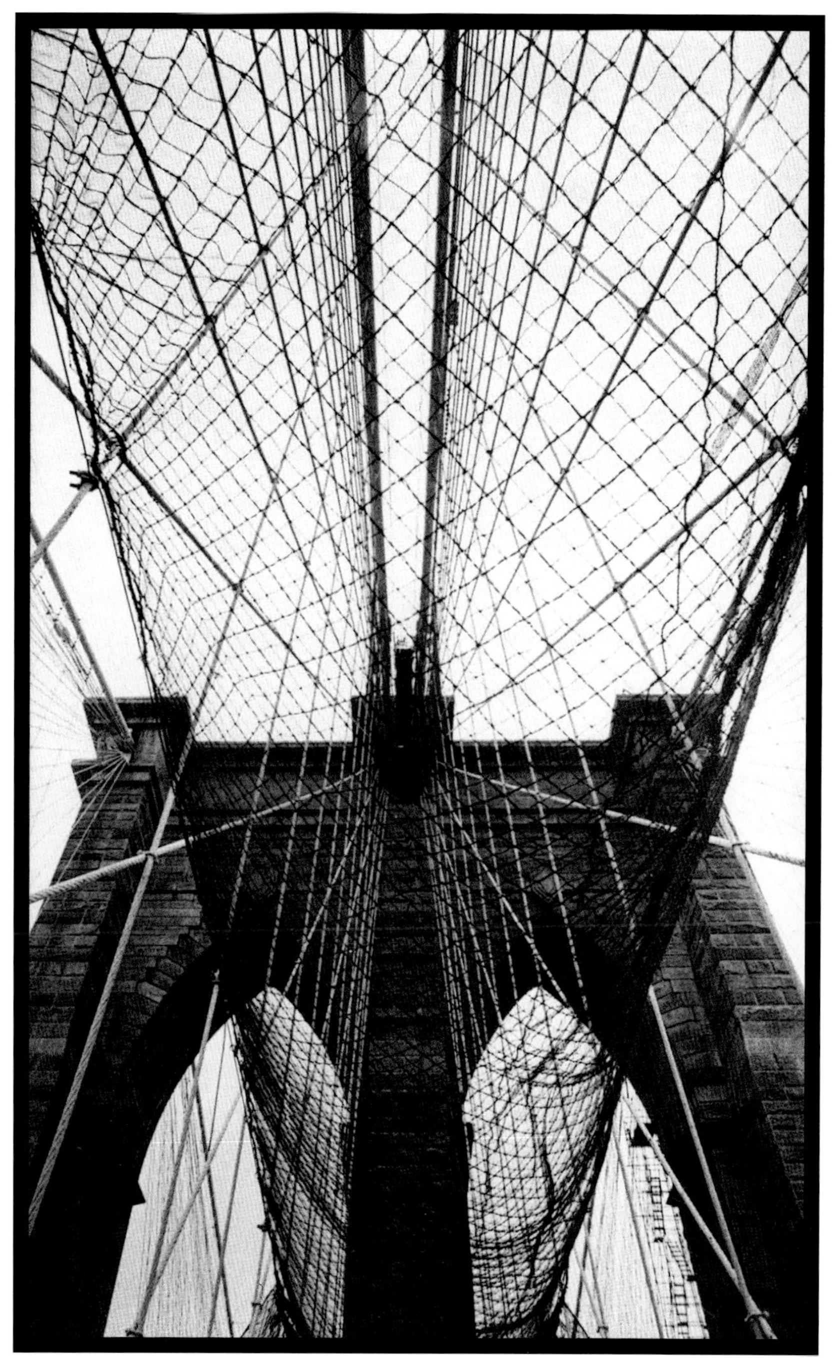

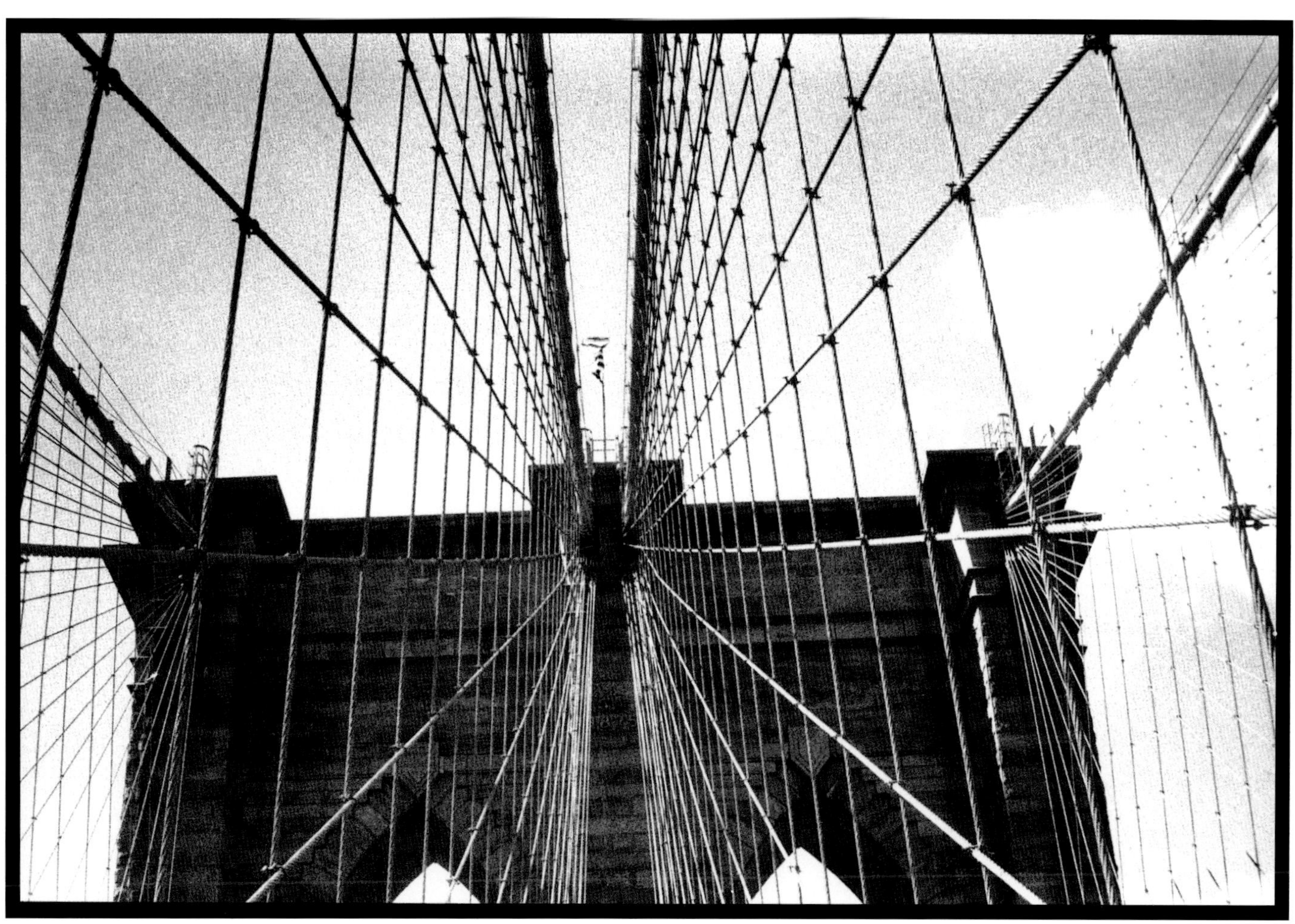

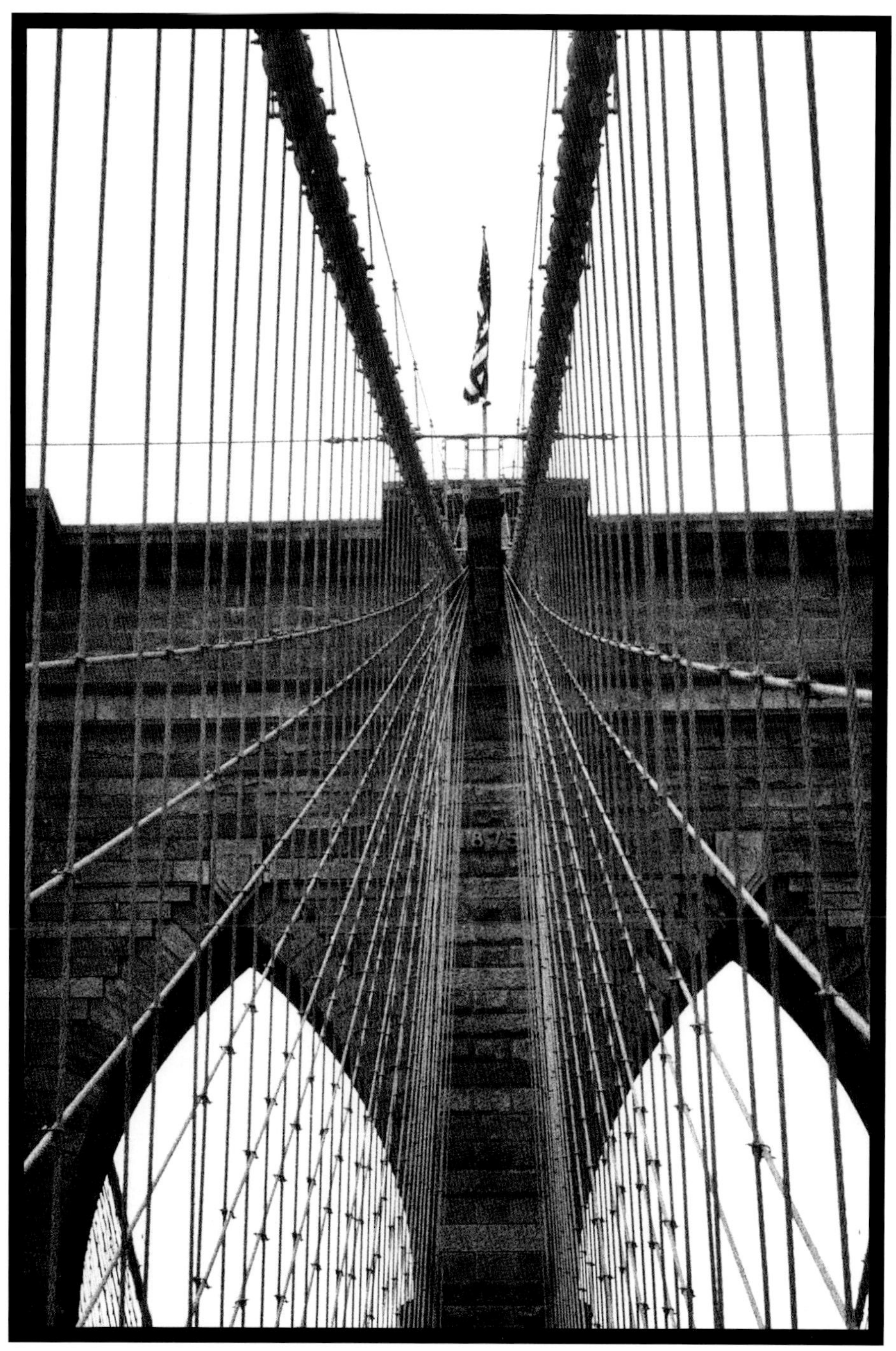

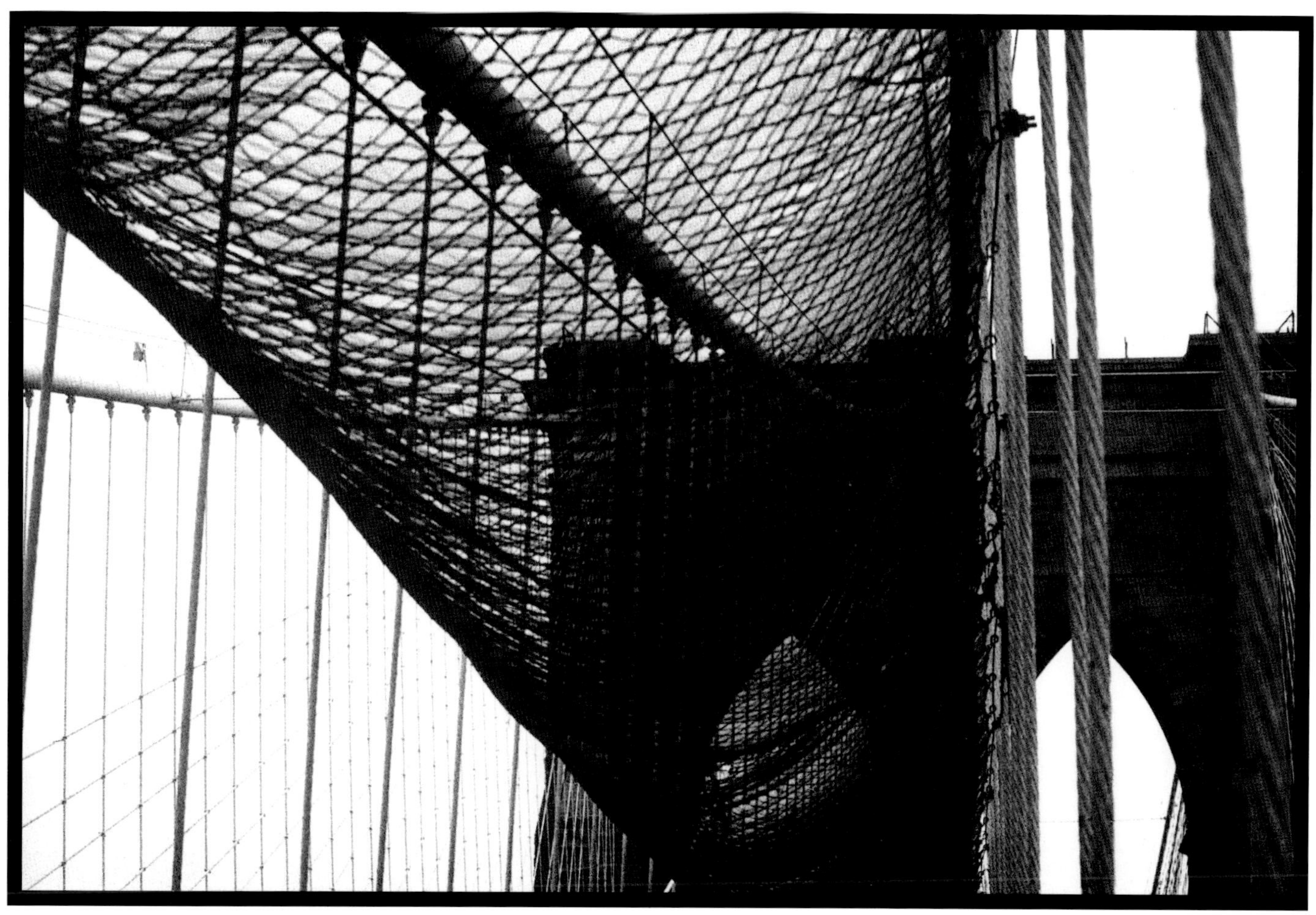

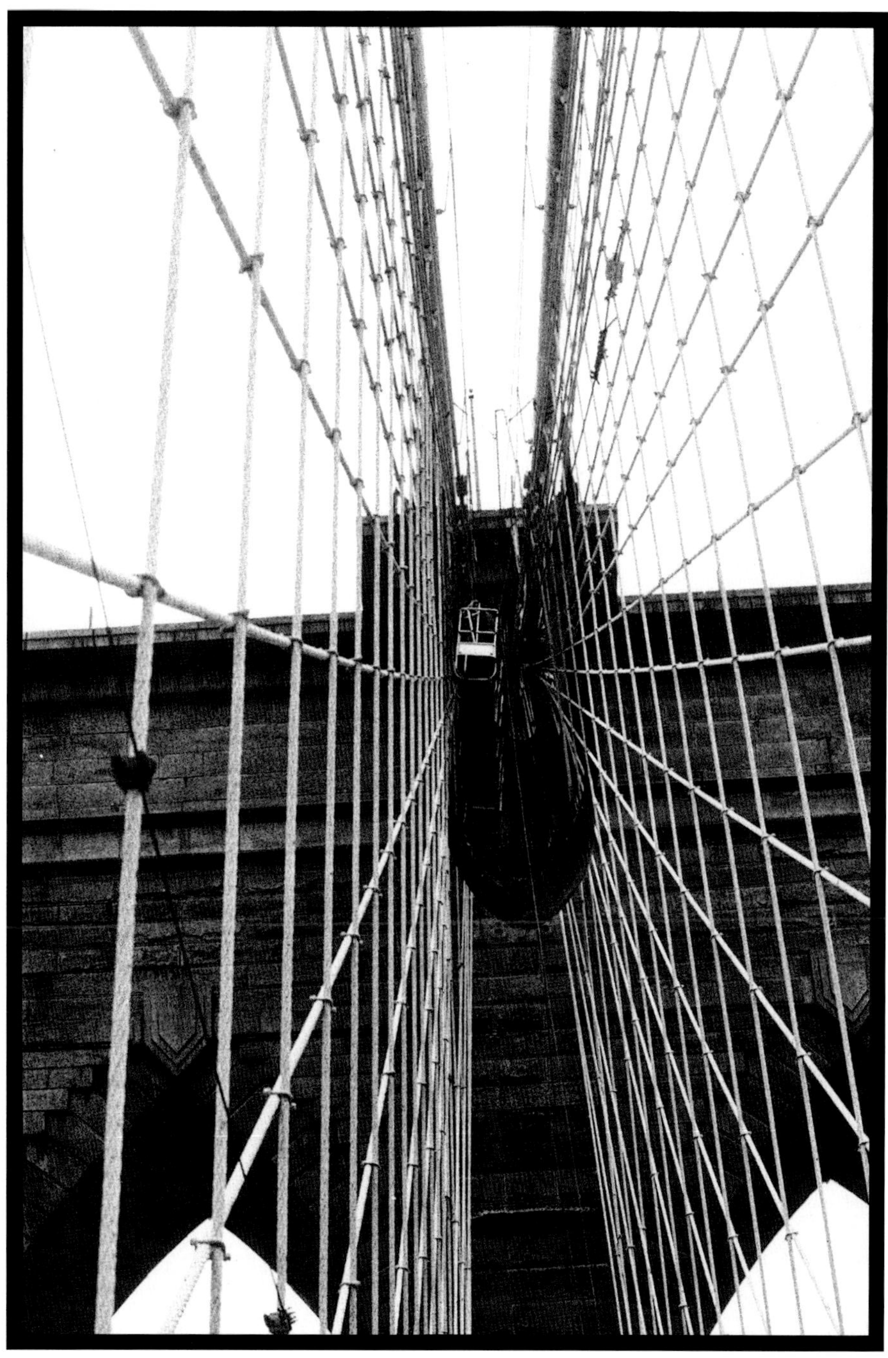

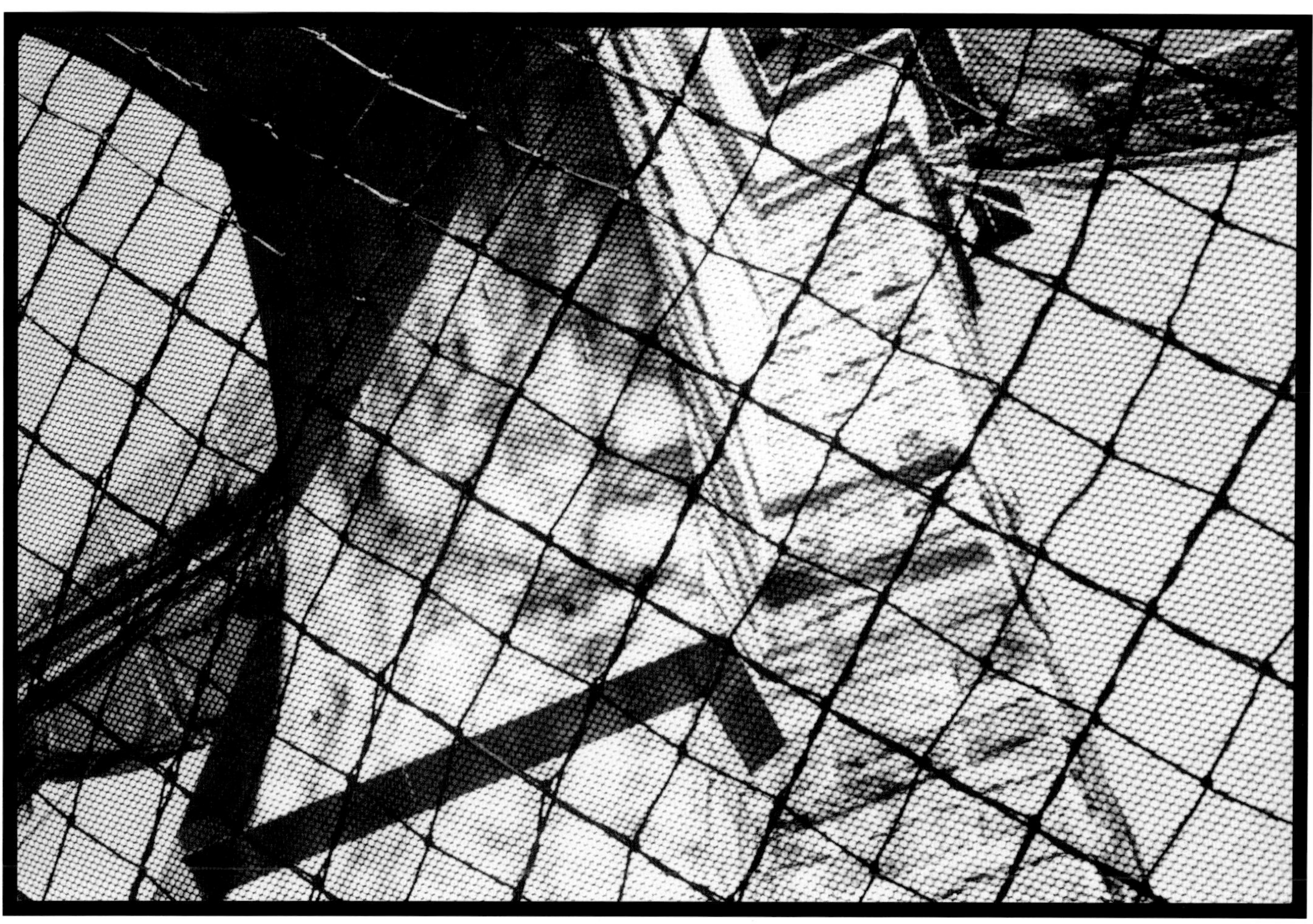